2040 9100 354 932 2

WITHDRAWN

D1543351

BOONE COUNTY PUBLIC LIBRARY
BURLINGTON, KY 41005
www.bcpl.org

SEP 8 2004

DUCKS, GEESE and TURKEYS
for anyone

DUCKS, GEESE
and TURKEYS
for a n y o n e

Victoria Roberts
BVSc, MRCVS

Foreword by

Jonathan Dimbleby

Whittet Books

FOR JACK

Frontispiece: three-week-old ducklings – Black Indian Runner, White Indian Runner and Buff Orpington

First published 2002
Text © 2002 by Victoria Roberts
Photographs © 2002 by Michael Corrigan
Whittet Books Ltd, Hill Farm, Stonham Rd, Cotton, Stowmarket, Suffolk IP14 4RQ

Distributed in Canada and USA by Diamond Farm Book Publishers, PO Box 537, Alexandria Bay, NY 13607
(800) 481-1353
Fax: (800) 305-5138
http://www.diamondfarm.com

All rights reserved. No part of this publication may be reproduced, transmitted or stored in a retrieval system, in any form or by any means, without permission in writing from Whittet Books Limited.

The right of Victoria Roberts to be identified as the author of this work has been asserted in accordance with the Copyright, Designs and Patents Act 1988.

Acknowledgments
The helpfulness and patience of the following breeders during photography is gratefully appreciated: Peter Christon, Graham Hicks, Janice Houghton-Wallace, Jack Killeen, Stephanie Mansell, the Moorhouse Family, Richard Simms and Roy Sutcliffe.

Cataloguing in Publication Data
A catalogue record for this title is available from the British Library

ISBN 1 873580 56 8

Printed in Hong Kong by Wing King Tong

CONTENTS

FOREWORD

by Jonathan Dimbleby

I grew up with chickens, ducks, and geese. I took them very much for granted - except that is for the geese which were far too fierce to be ignored. When I left home I also left the birds behind. It is only in the last couple of years that chickens and ducks (not yet geese) have come back into my life: Rhode Island Reds for their eggs and Indian Runners for the sheer delight of watching them about their daily lives in and around the pond.

For those of us who are born-again bird-lovers Victoria Roberts is a vital source of inspiration. She is a scholar who wears her learning lightly and who also has a delicious sense of humour. Her first book, *Poultry For Anyone*, succeeded triumphantly in being a beginner's guide that also enthralled the specialist. The same is true of *Ducks, Geese and Turkeys for Anyone*.

The text is simple, clear, and informative. In each case, she tells you the history of the breed; its characteristics (her detailed and humorous observations here are especially telling); its utility (unhappily - in the age of industrial agriculture - too often very limited except for niche or specialist markets); and, importantly, its 'special requirements'. These insights are illuminated by a beautiful set of photographs by Michael Corrigan.

For myself, I can think of few greater delights than to be perched on my window seat watching the ducks weaving and bobbing their way round the pond in the field outside while browsing my way through this excellently produced and immensely enjoyable work of love and scholarship.

Jonathan Dimbleby
December, 2001

PREFACE

Following on from the success of *Poultry for Anyone*, I felt it was a natural progression to write about ducks, geese and turkeys. As I have bred, judged and shown all these breeds over the past 28 years, I have come to know and love their various foibles and if people are interested either in first time keeping or adding another breed to their collection, I hope this book will help them make an informed decision, suiting their needs. All the popular breeds of ducks, geese and turkeys are covered in this volume, together with useful Appendices on management and health (I now find it difficult to resist the veterinary slant). It is particularly pleasing to see the recent formation of the Turkey Club UK and its enthusiastic promoters. Coloured or pure breed turkeys have long been a neglected part of poultry keeping, but fortunately have kept their devotees over the years.

The wonderful photographs are once again taken by Michael Corrigan, most of them in natural settings, and I am grateful to those breeders who endured the descent of us two slightly batty individuals, wanting to immortalise their best birds in all weathers.

Ducks, Geese and Turkeys for Anyone will, I hope, point you in the right direction for a lifelong interest in these fascinating birds.

Victoria Roberts BVSc MRCVS, 2001

Eight-week-old Black Indian Runners and Orpingtons.

INTRODUCTION

Ducks, geese and turkeys have probably been domesticated just as long as chickens, the earliest mention being around 1000 BC, but would have existed for hundreds of years only in the original form, without the variety of shapes and colours we know today as the birds would have been strictly utilitarian.

Mallard ducklings, if confined, would have contributed to the pot, and eggs would have been eagerly sought in the spring. Geese were useful in other ways. The greylag goose tames very easily and would have appreciated the odd bit of extra grain in cold weather. Their down, the soft and warm under layer of feathers, which they need to keep warm, was used in bedding and clothing and in eastern Europe in the past few hundred years was a major contributor to the economy, by which time the size had increased enormously through selection and white birds had been developed from sports. The strong primary feathers were also useful in that not only did they make good quill pens for the few that could write, mostly in the monasteries, but also arrows were sped on their way in a true line if three fletchings (feathers attached to the tail of an arrow to help guide it, like the tail of an aeroplane) were added from the feather. Hence being a fletcher was an important trade when arrows were one of the few weapons for war and hunting. Wild geese moult in the months of June and July and tend to do so in a quiet area in a large protective flock as at this stage they cannot fly. Collecting large amounts of primaries would have been easy if the flocks were near to habitation, but generally were not. Much better to have your own flock of larger geese which could not fly and therefore dropped their feathers in a convenient place, plus giving a ready supply of meat and eggs. The flocking instinct of ducks, geese and turkeys makes them relatively easy to drive if done slowly, and they are trainable to go in the hut on command at night, for instance. The Egyptians also had a soft spot for geese, these being depicted in various hieroglyphs and known from the beginning as being good watchdogs. As all waterfowl can sleep with half their brain at a time, there is always one on effective guard duty. Geese, particularly, recognise their human family and will shout indignantly if strangers appear: it is said that they will only take food from people they know. It is to be expected that ganders will guard their geese in the breeding season from both humans and other geese, but are generally not aggressive to people.

The Aztecs were responsible for taming the turkey as this was a good local source not only of meat and eggs but of wonderful ceremonial feathers. Many artefacts and place names attest to this in Mexico and then when the birds were brought to Europe in 1524, another useful bird was added to the growing list of domestications.

Of course, the various shapes, sizes and colours of all three species were developed by the Victorians as they not only had a penchant for something different, but also easy travel was suddenly made possible by the advent of the railways, plus the rapidly expanding seafaring expertise. Locally developed strains of birds would have taken slightly different forms, thus contributing to the incredible development of the humble mallard and greylag into the wide variety available today. Competitive exhibiting became popular in the 1850s and although it waned in the middle of the 19th century, has revived again, which has meant that some of the rarer or more unusual breeds are still available. The Poultry Club, which has been in existence since the first Standards were produced in 1865, is the guardian of the Standards. The latest edition of *The British Poultry Standards*, published by Blackwells in 1977, contains all the details judges and breeders need to know about the points of each breed and has colour photographs for the first time. The Poultry Club is an active organisation for both utility breeds and exhibition breeds (contact this publisher for the current Poultry Club Secretary), holding a show in December each year with currently over 6,000 entries of chickens, ducks, geese and turkeys.

There is also still a huge industry of meat, egg and feather production around the world of ducks, geese and turkeys.

Following on from the description and photographs of all the popular breeds, there are several Appendices containing useful information. Waterfowl and turkey keeping, like chicken keeping, is quickly addictive, so concise management guidelines will help you to expand your flock without too much conflict. Which breeds have certain practical uses is also provided so that you can choose the one most suited to your needs and pleasure.

DUCKS

*Wild mallard (*Anas platyrhynchos platyrhynchos*) in full breeding colour. All domestic ducks except the Muscovy are descended from these.*

ABACOT RANGER

Standard colours: one

History

Starting as a sport from the Khaki Campbells (see page 26) around 1917, this breed has had a chequered career, as not only was there disagreement on what colour it should be, there were other breeds or crossbreeds around with similar colouration adding to the confusion. Oscar Gray developed the sport primarily as a laying breed with the introduction of white Indian Runner ducks and named them after his duck ranch in Essex. They took part in laying trials competitions in 1922 and beat the Buff Orpingtons (see page 26) and most of the Runner pens. They were not Standardised at this time, but fortunately some birds were introduced to Germany in 1926. These bred to a stable colour eventually and were named Streicher-enten (Ranger ducks). It was only in the 1980s that these birds were noticed as being the same as the Abacot Ranger and the German Standard was adopted by The Poultry Club in 1987.

Current position

Popular for exhibition plus laying and meat, this pretty and active medium-sized breed has a bright future with many breeders.

Characteristics

The carriage is slightly upright and the birds should be alert and busy, with a well rounded body, the back and abdomen being almost parallel. The colour of the drake is a dilute mallard colour with a green head ending in a complete white neck ring. The breast is a rich red-brown with silver-white lacing. The belly, flanks and stern are white and the back is dark grey with white lacing. The wing bar (speculum) is important and should be violet in colour with white borders. The duck looks as though she has a rich buff sock on her head, this marking being known as a hood. Her body has a cream background streaked with light brown with the speculum being the same as the drake's. Her bill is slate colour and her legs are dark grey, whereas his bill is yellowish green with a black bean at the tip and his legs are dark orange – they both have dark brown eyes. The ducklings are yellow with dark 'guard hairs' giving them a smoky appearance until they get their adolescent feathers. There should not be any suggestion of an eye stripe. The ducklings grow fast and appreciate plenty of room to roam as they are basically a foraging breed.

Utility aspects

As mentioned above, this breed is a very good layer, but is still rounded enough to be useful for meat. With the pale underdown they pluck out clean white and with weights of 5½-6lb (2.5-2.7kg) for the drakes and 5-5½lb (2.25-2.5kg) for the duck any spare birds make a useful addition to the diet. At least you know what they have been fed on and how they have lived.

Abacot Ranger. The drake has not quite coloured up on his head which should be iridescent green.

Special requirements

These birds need lots of space to free-range with access to fresh water, not necessarily a pond. They do not take kindly to being kept in a small area, and will reward you with lots of very tasty eggs if they are allowed to forage as well as enhancing an area with their beauty.

AYLESBURY

Standard colours: white

History

Any large white duck is automatically called an Aylesbury as the English town was where the meat duck industry was established in the early 1700s with most of the then population being involved in growing the ducks for the lucrative London markets, boosted by the advent of the railways. The close conditions they were kept in tended to be less than hygienic and they were not allowed outside as they fattened quicker with intensive rearing. However, by the end of the 1800s, other faster growing meat breeds had been introduced (see also Pekin, page 47) and so the birds gradually became exhibition birds. A keel was developed to distinguish them from the other heavy white breeds and the Standard of 1905 states that six-month-old ducklings should not be less than 9lb (4kg) for the duck and 10lb (4.5kg) for the drake. When the birds reached their second year they were expected to be over 11lb (5kg). Left in the hands of only a few breeders, this magnificent breed has reached the stage of rarity. Commercial meat ducks are yellow billed, more upright, not as heavy and are not Standardised so no classes are put on for them at shows.

Current position

Due to the difficulty in maintaining size, breeders of Aylesburies are few but dedicated – some might even say obsessive. Most are kept for conservation and exhibition purposes but they are fast becoming a rare breed and a specialist club is planned to boost interest in them.

Characteristics

The massive rectangular white body, wedge-shaped head with long pink bill, blue eyes high up in the skull, straight head profile and short orange legs are not everyone's idea of beauty and grace, but if these ducks are given space to exercise, they are really quite agile. The back should be horizontal, with the keel parallel to the ground, but their wings cannot cross over the rump like other ducks due to the size of the body. Their legs should be centrally placed and they need to be fit to excel in the show pen: they have an infuriating habit of moulting if they even hear the mention of entry to a show. Training them to get used to a show cage reduces the stress and thus the level of moulting, but to get an Aylesbury in full feather is quite an art as they are loose feathered at the best of times. They need to be kept out of the sun to keep the bill pink for exhibition and appear to have skin two sizes too large. The very largest birds can have difficulty mating and fertility tends to be rather low with limited egg production in the spring – the duck looks as though she has to lay her eggs 'uphill'. Ducklings are bright yellow and need extra care and feeding to attain the maximum size. Due to this exaggeration of size, they tend not to live beyond five years and, like most ducks, are not good sitters. Definitely not a beginner's breed.

Aylesbury duck.

Utility aspects

Apart from one family firm rearing Aylesburies for meat with less keel, the breed is used entirely for exhibition. Of course spare drakes may be eaten and eggs not used for hatching are appreciated in the kitchen.

Special requirements

Extra care and feeding is needed for the rearing of the young to attain maximum size without excess protein and plenty of exercise is needed for ducklings and adults alike.

BALI

Standard colours: any colour permitted

History

First seen in 1925 as imports from Malaya by the Misses Davidson and Chisholm, the Bali looks like a crested Indian Runner duck (see page 35) but less upright. It has been known in Bali (an island east of Java) for hundreds of years, with a high production of white eggs. Standardisation was achieved in 1930, but the breed seemed to lose popularity after this. The breed was re-created in the 1980s from Crested and Indian Runners and is now more frequently seen at the shows.

Current position

In few hands, although the popularity seems to be increasing as show entries increase.

Characteristics

The birds should be erect and active with the body slim and cylindrical. The Bali resembles an Indian Runner with a wedge-shaped head, flat on top and slim neck and body, but the carriage is not as upright and the Bali has heavier shoulders. Although any colour is permissible, the white is popular and saxony (see Saxony, page 54), apricot, blue-fawn and brown have been produced. Symmetry of markings is important in the coloured birds. The crest is small and globular and is set rather on the back of the narrow head. As with all crested ducks, the genetics ensure that not all birds bred have crests but only those with crests may be exhibited. Sometimes it can be useful to breed a crestless bird (but bred from crested birds) back to a crested bird to fix other characteristics. A large crest seems to encourage broad shoulders, so remember that the body should not become so heavy as to resemble a Crested duck (see page 31). The sizes and weights are similar to the Indian Runner.

Utility aspects

Bali ducks lay very well, usually a white egg. They are also useful on the table as they are not as slim as Indian Runners. They are active foragers.

Special requirements

Plenty of room is needed for these active ducks. They do not need a pond but fresh water is essential to keep their heads and eyes clean. Beware in the spring if they lose weight while mating that they do not fly over fences and do some surreptitious cross mating.

Bali drake.

BLACK EAST INDIAN

Standard colours: black

History

Known in the UK since the mid 1800s, no-one could decide where these iridescent little bantam ducks originated. Variously called Buenos Aires, Labrador and Black Brazilian, the final name is probably the least accurate, but they were kept both at London Zoo and Knowsley Park at first. Several importations were made from an unrevealed place in the 'Indies' and so the name stuck. The breed is described in the first Book of Standards in 1865 and has been bred extensively since. Some think it is a black sport from the mallard: the shape is certainly similar. It was used to enhance the colour of the Cayuga (page 29).

Current position

Popular on the show bench and liked by breeders for the small and neat shape. A challenge to exhibit as birds over a year old tend to develop white feathers and once this happens they cannot be shown.

Characteristics

This is a busy, lively little duck with a slightly elevated carriage from the horizontal and a similarity in shape to the mallard but more compact. It is the colour, however, which makes this breed stand out from the crowd. The black is overlaid with a lustrous beetle-green sheen in both males and females, although the males tend to be slightly greener and any brown or purple in the plumage is a defect at any age, the drakes sometimes gaining a brown tinge as they get older. The head is neat and round with a high skull and the bill is set in a straight line from the top of the eye. The most lustrously green birds tend to not have a black bill, so it is challenging to strike a balance as the colour of the bill should be black, avoiding either yellow or green, with the legs as dark as possible. The shape of the bill is important: a flat bill with exaggerated serrations is to be avoided. As mentioned above, the breed is prone to producing white feathers as it gets older. Any bird less than a year old with white in it will not be at the top of the breeder's list. If, as sometimes happens, an older bird becomes completely white (particularly the females), with succeeding years it will be readily distinguishable from other white ducks as the eyes will remain dark brown, other white ducks and geese having blue eyes. The drake should weigh 2lb (0.9kg) and the duck $1\frac{1}{2}$-$1\frac{3}{4}$lb (0.7-0.8kg) – this means they are small enough to fly so will need either pinioning at day old or the feathers of one wing clipping once a year. Quite a talking point with this breed is that when they come into lay, the egg shells start off almost black, fading to dirty white as the clutch is completed. The ducklings hatch a dull black and once feeding, rear quite easily, but with so few eggs in comparison to larger breeds, young stock is not as readily available.

Pair of Black East Indian. They have not quite moulted through: the iridescent green should be all over.

Utility aspects

Not really useful for the table due to its size and black skin and egg production is normally restricted to one or two clutches in the spring. This breed is mostly used for exhibition, but also kept as an attractive ornamental addition to a garden. Being small, the ducks are good at slug control without doing too much damage to plants.

BLUE SWEDISH

Standard colours: blue

History
Blue ducks were mentioned in mid Victorian times in the poultry books, but it seems that Holland, Germany and Belgium developed them into what we recognise today, all with local names from the various areas. As these ducks were developed in various places, they differ slightly in colour and pattern, but the Standardised one in the UK is the Blue Swedish and is probably closest to the German version, the Gimbsheimer, which was developed in the early 1960s. This established the lacing on the feathers which was a help in stabilising the notoriously unstable blue colour.

Current position
Always popular due to the striking colour, nevertheless this is a challenging breed for both the breeder and exhibitor.

Characteristics
Blue is not really a colour but the way we see the dark and light pigments. It is unstable, as anyone who has come across the Andalusian chicken will understand. When blue is mated to blue, 50% come blue, 25% come black and 25% come silver, also known as splashed (a dirty grey/white), so 50% of the progeny are wasted from the point of view of showing. However, if the splashed and the blacks are mated together then all the progeny come blue, so it is worth keeping well shaped specimens of the splash and black colours. Added to this difficulty is the presence of a white bib which is supposed to stay within defined limits (3 x 4", 7.5 x 10cm) but has a tendency to expand. Two of the outer primary flights are also white with the speculum as inconspicuous as possible. The bill should be blue in both sexes. Body colour is an even slate blue, strongly laced with a darker shade and the drake has a slightly darker blue head with a greenish tinge. The white bib is an inverted heart and should not extend as far as the bill which should be dark blue in both sexes. Legs and webs are orange-black in the drake and blue-brown in the duck and eyes are brown in both. Despite being a large breed with drakes 8lb (3.6kg) and ducks 7lb (3.2kg), they are very agile and love nothing better than fossicking about for insects. The body should be held slightly above the horizontal with a nicely rounded abdomen: any hint of a keel is to be avoided. The ducklings hatch with their body colour and bib in place, so any culling can be done at this stage if needed. They are easy to rear.

Utility aspects
Spare drakes will fatten well and of course with the blacks and splashes not used for breeding there is a useful source of meat and eggs. They are a bit large to keep slugs down in the vegetable garden as their digging capabilities are remarkable. Egg production is quite good with white eggs, but limited to spring and summer.

Flock of Blue Swedish. The bib size does vary and in the centre is one of the silver ducks normally produced with black ones in this breed.

Special requirements

Blue Swedish need plenty of room to fulfil their ranging needs. Drakes are active, so need at least three ducks to avoid over-mating of the females with attendant feather loss. Feed needs to be maintained in the summer as keeping the birds in good condition when they are so active is not easy when the days are long.

CALL

Standard colours: white, apricot, grey (or mallard), silver, blue-fawn, magpie, bibbed, pied.

History

Tame ducks have been used to entice wild mallard into decoys for centuries in England and Holland. The word decoy comes from the Dutch for the trap they invented to catch these wild birds, *de kooi*. All ducks are eminently trainable and there may well have been a tame strain to return to the lake every night for food and then lead the wild birds into the hoop and net tunnels. The small ducks with a loud quack were known as Decoy ducks and developed supposedly by the Dutch, although some sources believe the ducks arrived from the Far East almost ready-made around 1800. People call any small duck a Call or Decoy duck and there are coloured, free flying, smaller than mallard size but still mallard shaped ducks available. These are not the Standardised birds, however, so caution needs exercising when buying unseen. Having been in the first book of Standards in 1865, they were then not included until 1982 when Dutch imports had renewed the interest in and popularity of these birds.

Current position

Immensely popular not only for their shape and character but the wide variety of colours available with individual classes at big shows sometimes reaching three figures. With the perennial temptation to produce new colours, the future of these little birds is assured.

Characteristics

See a white exhibition Call duck and immediately be transported back to bath time with the cute and round toy rubber ducks we all loved. Hear a female endlessly quacking without appearing to draw breath and wonder where the off switch is. But

Call ducks swimming amicably on a pond outside the breeding season.

White Call duck

do not be fooled by their cuddly appearance. These bright and alert ducks have attitude and can often be found bullying much larger birds if their territory is invaded. They are also very choosy concerning mates, so with the low egg production it is sensible to let them choose their own as they are likely to have nothing to do with the mate you choose especially for them. The carriage should be nearly level with the short legs set in the middle of the body which is small and compact, broad and deep. The head is neat and round with a high skull and very short bill set squarely into the head. The maximum length of the bill is 1¼"(3.1cm) but the better show birds have much shorter bills than this. The overall effect is a chubby bird with a largish round head with big round eyes – the baby features us humans are programmed to be attracted to instantly. Shape and weight are linked as a rangy, large-boned bird may be the correct weight but the wrong shape: drakes should be 20-24oz (570-680g) and ducks should be 16-20oz (450-570g).

The colours are many and varied. The white is probably the most popular and must be unsullied white with clear yellow bill (black spots tend to appear on females' bills with age), yellow legs and blue eyes. The original colour was probably the grey and is the wild mallard colour and pattern in both duck and drake, colours deriving from the mallard pattern retaining the eye stripe. The pied is basically mallard coloured but with symmetrical amounts of white on the neck and body and the silver is also basically mallard coloured but with white evenly dispersed throughout the feathering giving an overall much paler look. The magpie is just as difficult as the Magpie (page 40) duck to get the markings even on cap and back and the bibbed is similar to the Blue Swedish (page 20) in colour and markings. More popular

Blue Fawn Call drake.

Pied Call duck.

Dark Silver Call drake showing a very good head.

colours include the blue-fawn where it looks as though the brown of the mallard female is replaced by blue and the drake has the mallard pattern but with a blue head, claret breast and blue body. The apricot was developed from the blue-fawn and the duck is a lovely shade of apricot throughout with light grey on the back and wings and the drake has a steel blue head, incomplete white neck ring, light claret breast and light grey body – a paler version of the blue-fawn drake. Other colours are being developed or imported and put forward for Standardisation.

Breeding from the better exhibition birds is not easy. The exaggeratedly small size does appear to limit fertility and the low number of eggs adds to this. The incubation time is around 26 days. The ducklings are tiny and best reared without other breeds as they can be fragile and starter crumbs are sometimes too large and have to be crushed up. Call ducks fly very well and so they are all either pinioned at a few days old or the primary feathers clipped once a year. They tend to be home loving, so even if full winged will probably come back to where they were reared. Check that new stock has at least been clipped before letting them out, however, unless keeping them in an aviary type pen with a roof. Some breeders let them hatch out their own eggs as they are good mothers.

Utility aspects

Considered to be purely ornamental, there are insufficient eggs to eat as most go for breeding, and they are such individuals that eating them seems just not right.

Special requirements

Low flock numbers when rearing; consideration given to their capacity to fly; together with allowance for individuality will ensure that these birds are a pleasure to keep, breed and enjoy the huge competition at shows.

BOONE COUNTY

3649322

CAMPBELL

Standard colours: khaki, white, dark

History

At the turn of the 20th century only certain breeds of ducks were good layers. In 1902 Mrs Campbell from Uley in Gloucestershire crossed Indian Runners (page 35) and Rouens (page 51) with the intention of producing an active duck which laid well, was easy to rear with some meat qualities and looked more like a traditional duck than the upright Runner. After several years' selection and the infusion of wild mallard, an egg-laying machine was developed and once the colour was stabilised, given the catchy name of Khaki Campbell, influenced not only by the colour of the duck but by the then patriotism for the military heroes. The Abacot Ranger (page 12) was an offshoot of this experimental breeding as was the Welsh Harlequin (page 61). Mrs Campbell resisted for years the Standardisation of the breed as she was of the opinion that once in exhibitors' hands, the breed would lose its main utility points. The White was developed around 1924 by Captain Pardoe so that it would still produce large numbers of eggs plus be crossed to produce a meat breed which would pluck clean. The White and Dark were first Standardised in the 1950s and the latter was developed by Mr Humphreys of Devon as a sex-linked breed. This means if a Khaki male is mated to a Dark female the ducklings hatch with dark down if they are male and pale down if they are female. This attribute was not as popular as other auto-sexing poultry breeds as ducks are easy to vent sex at up to 4 weeks (see page 118) or can be sexed by their voices at about 6 weeks old, unlike chickens where 10 weeks is often the earliest time to sex the plain coloured breeds. The commercial Khaki Campbell was then produced in huge numbers by the Dutch firm of Kortlang in Kent and they still send ducklings all over the world.

Current position

The Khaki is well established as a utility bird but some show specimens have become over large. The White is in fewer hands, but popular as the 'Jemima Puddleduck' inspiration and frequently seen at the larger shows. The numbers of the Dark are low in comparison.

Characteristics

This is a very active breed with a slightly upright carriage and the head carried high. The body is deep and wide and the abdomen of the female is well developed. The overall effect should be of a refined bird, but a worker all the same. The colour of Khaki was originally based on the dust-coloured light soils and withered grass of India: the Standard asks for 'a warm khaki' but does not define the colour, so it tends to vary between strains. The drake has head, neck, stern and wing bar of green-bronze with khaki elsewhere and a slaty brown bill. The duck is subtly laced with a slightly darker shade of khaki on an even shade of warm khaki with a dark bill. Both sexes have brown eyes and khaki legs. The White is pure white with clear yellow bill and legs and blue eyes in both sexes. The Dark is a darker version of the Khaki and none of the colours should show an eye stripe with any white on the Khaki or the Dark being a major fault. With the large amount of eggs, hatching can be arranged

Trio of Khaki Campbells.

Pair of Dark Campbells.

White Campbells heavy in lay.

to suit during the year, but make sure that one drake has several females to avoid injury from over mating. The ducklings are hardy, rear easily and if socialised at an early age get quite tame. The eggs of the Khaki are always white, but some strains of White Campbell lay blue eggs, as do some Darks. The drakes should weigh 5-5½lb (2.25-2.5kg) and the ducks in laying condition 4½-5lb (2-2.25kg). It is rare for any Campbell to go broody and even if they do, they are not trustworthy to sit and should be moved to another pen to break the broody cycle as they lose weight very quickly and then take a while to start laying again.

Utility aspects

Egg laying mainly, but there is sufficient meat on confined young drakes to be useful. If not confined they tend to be rather scrawny as they are so active. A good breed for beginners as they are so productive – prizes will be won if cakes are made with duck eggs, although they are an acquired taste boiled as the whites are rather rubbery.

Special requirements

Plenty of space as these ducks are first class foragers. If not let out until 9am they will lay in the hut rather than at random in the grass or in water.

CAYUGA

Standard colours: black

History
Several authors agree that the Cayuga originated in North America in New York State. There is a wild black duck and it was thought as early as 1809 that these were the antecedents of the Cayuga, but others think that the wild mallard was involved. They were first seen in the UK in the mid 1800s. The original colour was improved by crossing with the Black East Indian (page 18) so that the green sheen was enhanced on the larger duck. The breed was used as a table duck and so size was more important than the colour, but with the trend towards exhibiting the colour has improved still further.

Current position
Not being as prolific as some breeds makes these ducks sometimes difficult to obtain, but they are popular for their colour of both feathers and eggs.

Characteristics
Despite its size this is a lively duck with a near horizontal carriage which should be clear of the ground with no keel. The body is long and deep with the black legs set midway and the head and black bill are long. The drake should weigh 8lb (3.6kg) and the duck 7lb (3.2kg) but it is not often that these weights are found in the show pen: the lustrous beetle-green colour in some strains has been improved at the expense

Pair of Cayuga.

of size and the most lustrous tend to have greenish bills. In older birds, especially drakes, the legs start to gain an orange tinge and there is the same problem as with the Black East Indian in that females start to moult white after about 2 years and the drakes get white feathers around the head. For breeding purposes therefore, choose two-year-old birds with the least white on them. With the sun on them Cayugas look magnificent and when judging them it is sensible to get them in natural light. Any birds which show brown or purple tinges should be removed from the breeding pen. The eggs (like the Black East Indian) are black coloured at the start of the clutch and then fade to dirty white but the contents are very edible, being most useful in cakes and puddings. The ducklings hatch black but some have a few white down feathers. Any young duck with white feathers at the next moult should not be used for breeding as white in the breed has been a recurrent problem over the years. The ducks will sometimes go broody and make reasonable mothers if they are patient enough to sit the full four weeks.

Utility aspects

Mis-marked birds make good table birds if confined although the skin is rather dark, and the colour of the eggs is a talking point, especially when in an egg box with white and blue eggs.

Special requirements

This breed needs a reasonable amount of space to forage but they seem adaptable and will put up with smaller quarters than some of the lighter ducks.

CRESTED

Standard colours: any colour is permitted
Bantam and large versions

History

This is one of the oldest types of domestic duck as several 17th century paintings by different artists depict them in various colours. They were probably popular then due to their extraordinary headgear, although wild waterfowl may occasionally produce the odd crested individual. After some popularity in Victorian times, the Crested was almost lost until the 1950s when John Hall found one source and bred up from them, making them a good bird for exhibiting. Earlier reports stressed their utility aspects both with eggs and meat. The Bali (page 16) is the only other Standardised crested breed.

Current position

Good Cresteds are delightful and unusual and with no restrictions on colour beginners have a chance at the shows, making them a popular breed.

Coloured Crested drake.

White Crested drake.

Flock of miniature Coloured Crested ducks.

Characteristics

The crest is the main attribute, although the body should be free of deformities such as a kinked neck, short or roach back or a wry tail. It is important to select against these common deformities as they are linked to the crested gene. Top breeders mate a drake with a large crest to an unrelated duck with a smaller but well-shaped crest to achieve more consistent results. The crest also carries a lethal gene which means that of a hatch, 25% are dead in shell. Another 25% have no crest and 50% are crested. So there is some wastage from the point of view of exhibiting especially as the quality of the crest can be seen at hatching, but these ducks are good layers and large enough to eat as well. The crest should be round and set evenly on the skull but not interfering with the eyes, with the front of the crest above the eye. It should not

Flock of miniature White Crested ducks.

be split, fall over to one side or slip down the neck. The drakes should weigh 7lb (3.2kg) and the ducks 6lb (2.7kg) but these weights are difficult to maintain as the breed is so active. The most common colours are pure white, Silver Appleyard (page 56) or any other colour so long as the markings are symmetrical.

The miniature Crested is the same as the larger version except in size when it should be 2½lb (1.1kg) in the drake and 2lb (0.9kg) in the duck, but it is more of a challenge to breed as the smaller a duck gets the less fertile it seems to be, adding to the problems of breeding with the crested gene. These were created in the late 1980s and are not often seen at the shows.

Utility aspects

The large Crested ducks are good layers and produce some meat. The plain headed or badly crested ones can always be useful for production, although not needed for breeding or showing. The miniatures just about lay enough to hatch a few.

Special requirements

Plenty of space is needed for these active ducks and make sure there are several females to one male as the crests and the ducks themselves are easily damaged by over mating.

INDIAN RUNNER

Standard colours: black, chocolate, fawn, fawn-and-white, mallard, trout, Cumberland blue, white

History

This classic Malayan egg producing breed was introduced into the UK in white, fawn-and-white and fawns in the mid 1800s, but the other colours were not Standardised until after 1906. For hundreds of years the ducks in the Far East were taken to the rice fields for weeding and insect control and then taken back to the village for safety at night. Obviously, a duck which could walk easily was selected and so the legs were set further and further back on the body until the stance was almost upright. In the marshy lands of south Java ducks were bred in their thousands and then walked to market when about 10 weeks old, a journey which could take months. Eggs and poor doers were sold *en route* so that stock which arrived at market was very fit and hardy. Several types were imported from various parts of Malaya, leading to argument over which was the 'correct' type. The word Indian in Victorian times was taken to mean the Indies, including India, Burma, Malaya and parts of the East and importers were understandably cagey as to the origin of their stock as they wished the price to remain high. Ducks were economically very important in South East Asia, much more so than in other parts of the world with eggs from Indonesia and meat ducks from China (see Pekin, page 47). The first Runners in the UK arrived in Cumbria but these were then bred with local ducks and lost some of the upright stance. Unfortunately, once Standardised, most points were allocated for markings rather than type, so it was a while before the upright type was

Flock of Trout Indian Runners. When the three drakes colour up they will be similar to a drake mallard.

White Indian Runner drake.

(RIGHT) *Pair of Fawn and White Indian Runners.*

re-established, although the earlier laying type was less upright than the modern exhibition ducks.

Current position

Kept by some people just because they make them smile, Runners have a devoted following whether for exhibition or egg production. Several spare drakes are needed for a decent meal, however.

Characteristics

Very different from other ducks, the comical Indian Runner is in a class of its own. The outline of a Runner duck should be like that of a nearly vertical walking stick with a slightly downward bent handle representing the head. The skull is flat and the eye is set as high as possible with the bill long and set in a straight line with the skull. The neck is long but should never be more than one third of the total height. The classic hock bottle shape is desired for where the neck and body join, with the shoulders being narrow and the body in the shape of a tube. The legs need to be set far back to allow for the upright stance, with the tail in a straight line with the back, but if the tail goes between the legs the bird overbalances and is not correctly proportioned. The typical action is a straight-out walk or run with no waddling.

The original colours are white: pure white with orange-yellow bill and legs and these tend to be slimmer than the other colours. Fawn is a warm ginger-fawn in the duck with red-brown pencilling and the drake has a dark bronze head melding with the rich brown-red of the neck and breast. The lower chest and abdomen is grey with the tail and wings dark brown. Bills and legs in both sexes are black or dark tan and an eye stripe is not allowed. The fawn-and-white has specifically defined coloured areas. The cap and cheek markings in the duck are the same shade as the body markings which reach from mid neck to mid abdomen and these feathers are pencilled. The tail is brown. The drake has a bronze-green cap and cheek markings with more finely pencilled body markings and a darker tail. The wings in both sexes are white with fawn coverts, giving a heart shape on the back. There is a white streak which reaches from the neck up to the eye and some white from under the chin to part way up the bill which starts yellowish in young ducks and then goes greener as the birds age, with legs orange-red. The American fawn-and-white is similar but with no pencilling.

Other later solid colours Standardised include the black which has a green sheen in both sexes and no white anywhere; the chocolate which is a rich solid chocolate with no lacing and the Cumberland blue which is not so much laced as shaded on each feather.

The Mallard Runner is, as its name implies, identical in markings to the wild mallard including eye stripes. The Trout is slightly lighter in shade than the Mallard with the belly of the duck giving the appearance of the mottling on a brown trout, and these have always been slightly smaller, finer and less upright than the other colours of Runners.

Weights are 3½-5lb (1.6-2.25 kg) in the drake and 3-4½lb (1.35-2kg) in the duck.

The best Indian Runner judges at shows put all the entrants in a class into the passageway and see how they run – any weak legs are immediately discovered, even though the bird may have looked wonderful in the show pen.

Flock of Fawn and White Indian Runners.

Due to the large numbers of eggs hatching can be done when convenient. The occasional duck will go broody but they are not trustworthy and the drakes can get positively vicious with ducklings. It is best to allow only one drake to several ducks to avoid damage due to over mating – the Runner is particularly enthusiastic and when he has lost weight in the Spring will fly over the fence to mate with any other breed, or indeed anything which stands still long enough. Ducklings will tame down if socialised from a young age, but adults can be very nervous otherwise and in a strange place run and hide until they get their bearings.

Utility aspects

Mainly eggs which vary from blue to white linked to the colour of the duck, although not as many eggs per year as the Khaki Campbell (page 26). There is a certain amount of breast meat with little fat as the birds are so active.

Special requirements

These birds are great foragers and thus need plenty of space. They are happy with a water dish as opposed to a pond as they prefer walking to swimming.

MAGPIE

Standard colours: black and white, blue and white, dun and white

History

There were black and white ducks in West Wales many years before they became fashionable, but much work was put into getting the markings right and a Club was formed in 1926. Magpies also partook in laying trials, but trailed behind the Campbells and Runners. The black and white and the blue and white were accepted by the Club early on, with the dun and white appearing later. It was not until 1982 that the full Standard was published but then only for the black and white and by 1997 all three colours were included. The Magpie has always intrigued fanciers as the correct markings of the breed are difficult to obtain, especially on the ducks, and so exhibitors generally have a good flock of 'utility' ducks with only a few worth showing.

Current position

With good utility points this breed will always have a place, but fanciers need to be almost obsessive to produce good show specimens.

Black and White Magpie drake.

Flock of Blue and White Magpies.

Characteristics

A broad, deep and long body enables this duck to be an excellent forager with a carriage of about 35°. The long back and long neck give it a racy appearance but still well proportioned. The head is also long with a large, bright alert eye. When, as happens, sometimes all white Magpies are hatched with a batch of say, Campbells, the only way to tell them apart is this long and racy outline. The symmetrical markings should be a coloured cap above the eyes and a coloured heart-shape from the shoulders to the tip of the tail, all else being white. This is more difficult to achieve on the ducks than the drakes and as the ducklings hatch with the coloured areas already apparent, it is easy to select good ones at day old. They are strong and easy to rear. The bills should all be yellow, but older birds tend to develop a green hue. The eyes are dark and the legs orange. The drakes weigh 5½-7lb (2.5-3.2kg) and the ducks 4½-6lb (2-2.7kg) so there may be quite a variation in size. Penalties are imposed for excess weight, however, but it is not easy keeping weight on exhibition birds in the breeding season as they are so active. Experienced breeders like to mate birds together that complement each others' markings – a strong cap in the drake with a weak cap in the duck, for instance. This method also helps to reduce the defects of a dished bill, wry tail or coarseness, all needing to be selected against in this breed.

Utility aspects

Good for both meat and blue eggs, the mismarked birds can be confined and fattened or used as layers.

Special requirements

Despite being a good forager, the Magpie seems happy in confined spaces. Be prepared to cull or have other uses for mismarked birds.

MUSCOVY

Standard colours: black, white, blue (lavender), black and white, blue and white, white-winged black, white-winged blue

History

Wild Muscovies (*Cairina moschata*) are native to Central and South America and the family is a member of the perching duck classification. All other domestic ducks are descended from the mallard, but Muscovies have been domesticated since before the Spanish invaded South America in the 1500s. The wild version has much less of the typical caruncles on the face and tends to be smaller and mostly black in colour. The South American Indians developed the birds for both meat and eggs, and of course the birds were happy in their natural climate. The domestic version is much larger and comes in many different colours but still likes to perch.

Current position

Valued for their meat and egg production plus broody capacity, the numbers of this breed are high.

Characteristics

As Muscovies are not descended from the mallard, they lack the 'sex curls' that are present on all other adult domestic duck drakes. The carriage of both male and female is horizontal with the legs set centrally and they are supposed to be jaunty with a wild or fierce expression. This gives a clue to their character: Muscovies can be aggressive to other ducks and the males enjoy fighting amongst themselves. Both

Black and White Muscovy drake with good caruncles.

Muscovy duck with her own ducklings.

males and females are extremely strong, so when handling them it is advisable to wear gloves and long sleeves as their long claws are very sharp. Having said that, the females particularly become very tame and are renowned for their broodiness and mothering ability. The incubation time of the slightly olive coloured eggs is 35 days (compared to 28 for other ducks) and Muscovies are happy sitting on their own eggs or other duck or goose eggs, but make sure that they are set so that all hatch together, i.e. set other duck eggs one week after the Muscovy eggs. The head of the male is large and there are red or black caruncles on the face over the base of the bill which is strong, slightly curved and varies in colour from yellow and black to red or flesh. The eyes are large and can range in colour from yellow to brown to blue, depending on plumage colour and legs are white to black. There is a small crest in both male and female which can be raised in alarm or excitement. The plumage colours of black, blue or chocolate can be solid or mixed with white, but the markings need to be symmetrical. Exhibition points for colour are only 10% of the total – the shape and carriage is the most important feature – so show birds tend to be the largest.

The ducklings are strong and easy to rear artificially, but have a tendency to pull feathers off other breeds, so it may be necessary to keep them separate and they start to graze at an early age, enjoying any insects or fish available. If vent sexing is not practised, the growing males quickly become much larger than the females and when adult are nearly twice the size with drakes at 10-14lb (4.55-6.35kg) and ducks 5-7lb (2.25-3.2kg). Both sexes have a keel, more pronounced in the male.

The Muscovy makes no noise except for a gentle hiss, usually accompanied by a forward and back head extension. If frightened, the female will make a sort of quack and she mutters quietly to her ducklings. Muscovies will sometimes mate with other domestic ducks but their progeny are mules, i.e. they are infertile.

There is much more meat on a Muscovy than other domestic ducks, both on breast and legs and with little fat, but plucking their three layers of feathers is not a job for the fainthearted – most people just skin the birds for the table.

Utility aspects

Prized for their succulent flesh, the Muscovy has been commercialised in France by crossing with the Pekin (page 47) to produce the Mullard (which is infertile) and this is also known as a Barbary duck. These have a fast growth rate, are less aggressive and have feathers easier to remove. Egg production tends to be in clutches, but continues through the spring and summer. The maternal instincts are utilised to hatch other breeds.

Special requirement

A fair amount of space with plenty of grass is needed. The females especially can fly very well, so either clip one wing or have a net over the pen. The males tend to be too heavy to stay off the ground for long. Remember that the incubation time is different and that this breed likes to perch both at night and during the day.

ORPINGTON

Standard colours: buff

History

This breed was created round the end of the 1890s by William Cook of Orpington in Kent, the man who also created the famous Buff Orpington chickens. The duck was intended to be dual purpose, laying well and large enough to produce a good carcase.

The ever-popular colour was much admired by other breeders, so much so that a Standard was drawn up around 1908. Unsurprisingly, the breed did not lay as well as the Campbells and Runners and there were two other colours produced at this time, the blue and the chocolate, both of which have subsequently been dropped from the Standards. Never as popular as the Khaki Campbell, perhaps due to not having such a catchy name, Buff Orpingtons have nevertheless maintained a devoted following over the years for those who like beauty and elegance combined with utility.

Quartet of Buff Orpingtons.

Frequently seen at the shows and certain lines have recently been vastly improved, becoming instantly recognisable from others.

Characteristics
The slightly upright carriage ensures good foraging ability, but the duck should have a well-developed abdomen, clear of the ground, when in lay. The body is broad, long and deep but without any sign of a keel. The breast is full and round and the tail is small. The head is fine and oval in shape and the bill is moderate in length with the bold eyes set high in the skull. Drakes should weigh 5-7½lb (2.25-3.4kg) and ducks 5-7lb (2.25-3.2kg) so there is plenty of scope for a well-fleshed carcase. It is the colour that attracts most attention, however. The drake's body is a rich even shade of red-buff throughout with no lacing or pencilling and the head and neck are glossy seal brown with no evidence of grey or green. The red-brown rump should have no blue on it. The bill is yellow with a dark bean and in both sexes the eyes are brown and the legs orange-red. The duck has the same rich red-buff body plumage, again with no lacing, eye-stripe or pencilling. The plumage should be free from blue, brown or white feathers and she has an orange-brown bill. The colour and the type hold equal show points, so there is much selection to be done for the show bench, especially as a mating of two correctly coloured birds will not result in 100% of the progeny being the correct colour. There is similar wastage to the Blue Swedish (page 20) as 25% will be light buff, 25% khaki and 50% the correct buff. As long as birds are selected for the least lacing and least blue shades, together with no white feathers and no grey or green in the head of the drake, some good birds should be bred. There are plenty of white eggs, but the duck is not dependable as a sitter. The ducklings hatch buff-coloured and are hardy and easy to rear. The drake does not get his full colour until about 5-6 months old and older females are likely to fade in the sun until they moult through again. Older drakes can go into an eclipse plumage on the head during the summer. They seem very sensible ducks and can get nicely tame.

Utility aspects
A true dual-purpose duck for both meat and eggs.

Special requirements
A fair amount of space is needed due to their foraging habits plus shade if birds are to be exhibited.

PEKIN

Standard colours: cream

History

Imported from China in 1872, these stout ducks have been bred in that country for many centuries. They were immediately a success in Victorian England not only with their fluffy, toy-like appeal but for their speedy meat production. The exhibition birds have become more upright over the years and these are not used for commercial production. The typical farmyard big-white-duck-with-a-yellow-bill which most people erroneously call an Aylesbury (page 14) has a much lower carriage and is bred and raised in thousands in Lincolnshire and Norfolk. Most of us are familiar with eating delicious crispy Pekin duck. Examples of the breed were also taken to America and Germany and the latter were bred more upright. Following importations in the 1970s from Germany, the show Pekin which we know today became more popular. The American version looks more similar to the commercial meat duck and we do not have a Standard for it here. The original colour in the Standard was buff canary, which proved impossible to attain, so deep cream or cream was settled on instead.

Flock of Pekin ducks.

Very popular due to their character plus meat production, the classes at shows are strong and there is good competition.

Characteristics
The shape of a good Pekin is likened to a nearly upright wide boat standing on its stern. They certainly remind one of those toys which are weighted at the base and cannot be knocked over. The almost upright carriage is elevated in the front and slopes down towards the rear. The body is broad and full with a slight keel between the legs and a broad, deep paunch and with the drakes weighing 9lb (4.1kg) and ducks 8lb (3.6kg). The stern is carried just above the ground with the tail carried high. The head is large, broad and round with a high skull and heavy cheeks. The bill is short and broad and the eyes appear shaded by heavy eyebrows. The long thick neck seems short due to the abundance of feather and is slightly gulleted at the throat. The legs are set well back to allow the upright carriage and the bill and legs in both sexes are bright orange. The plumage is very abundant and fluffy and when the feathers first come through they are a deep cream colour which then fades to a lighter cream. Because of all the fluff around the stern, the birds need to be kept in cleaner conditions than ducks with tighter feathering as they seem to pick up mud more easily. They also can have problems with their piggy eyes and if fresh water is not available for washing, infection quickly sets in. Some breeders put wheat in the bottom of the drinker so that the birds have to wash in order to eat. The ducks are so stout that when they sleep they pillow their heads on the ground – they cannot tuck them under their wings like other breeds. They are fairly active, despite their shape, but can be contained behind quite low fencing. The white eggs are most fertile from April and the ducklings rear well but need exercise to keep their legs strong. As the eggs are round, rather than egg-shaped, it is easy to set them in an incubator the wrong way up (they should have the air sac at the top) so some of the ducklings pip at the wrong end and need help to hatch out. The eggs need candling (shine a bright torch through the shell to see the air sac) either before setting or at one week to make sure they are the correct way up.

The only time I get deliberately bitten by ducks is when judging Pekins – they seem to like a good nibble and tweak of human skin and are strong enough to hang on. They don't do any serious damage, though. Faults to avoid when breeding or selecting for the shows are a double dewlap, crooked back and dished bill.

Utility aspects
Mainly bred for meat originally, they are mostly kept for exhibition purposes nowadays, but ones not good enough for showing do well in the pot.

Special requirements
Clean water is needed so that their eyes do not get infected and plenty of grass, not mud, is better so they stay cleaner.

ROUEN CLAIR

Standard colours: one, different from the Rouen

History

Although known in its native Normandy for many years and described in poultry books in the 1920s as a good utility duck, this breed did not enter the Standards until 1982, when there was a general resurgence in interest in domestic ducks with several new breeds imported. It was developed as a faster growing bird from the dark (*foncé*) Rouen and called the light (*clair*) Rouen.

Current position

A few birds are seen at shows and there is a dedicated core of breeders, but the number of birds is not high in the UK.

Characteristics

The bird should look like a huge mallard with the same long and racy outline. It should be 35in (90cm) from the point of the bill to the end of the tail with the neck extended. This tends to give it some grace, despite its size of $7\frac{1}{2}$-9lb (3.4-4.1kg) in the drake and $6\frac{1}{2}$-$7\frac{1}{2}$lb (3-3.4kg) in the duck. The carriage is slightly upright and there should be no keel in either sex. The bill of the drake is yellow with a green tint (no black lines are allowed on it) and the head and neck are green, ending in an incomplete white ring. The breast is red-chestnut with white edging to each feather and the grey flank finishes before the white stern. The back and wings are a darker

Pair of Rouen Clair. The drake on the right is in eclipse.

49

Rouen Clair drake in full colour.

shade than the flanks, the speculum is indigo (violet-blue) with a white border above and below and the rump is black. The eye is yellow in the drake and brown in the duck and legs in both sexes are yellow-orange. The head of the duck has the dark eye-stripe and head markings of the wild mallard, with a white eyebrow and a white line from the eye to the bill which is bright orange-ochre with a brown saddle. The throat is pale but these feathers must not extend on the breast. Body feathers are a dark fawn in colour with a dark brown 'V' shape on each one, reducing to a tick on the breast feathers. The flanks are slightly lighter in colour, but similarly patterned to the back with the grey wings and the speculum the same as the drake. Egg production is good in the warmer months and the ducklings are strong, rear easily and grow quickly, but the colour can vary slightly within a clutch due to their mixed ancestry. These are busy, active ducks with a good appetite.

Utility aspects
They were bred originally for meat and have a good carcase. Laying capacity is reasonable.

Special requirements
They need plenty of space to forage.

ROUEN

Standard colours: one, similar to the wild mallard

History

These ducks were developed in Normandy for the table and were known before 1750. They were not as large as later birds, but even by 1800, ten-week-old drakes were expected to reach 6lb (2.7kg). In those days they were kept in separate hutches and individually fed to increase the weight faster, therefore selecting for better growth. Rouens were introduced to the UK in the early 1800s and were then used for exhibition, with the size gradually being increased again. The Victorians loved extremes in all types of livestock and so these massive ducks remained popular, but became so closely inbred by the 1950s that most of the eggs were infertile. It was only after some imported ducks were used in the 1970s that the breed once again was seen on the show circuit.

Current position

Really only kept as exhibition stock, this is a specialist breed for those with more experience.

Characteristics

There is nothing quite like a flock of Rouens for size and colour. For all their vastness, with drakes at 10-12lb (4.55-5.44kg) and ducks at 9-11lb (4.10-4.98kg), they are remarkably strong and agile and will travel far in their search for insects but are easily restrained behind low fencing. The almost rectangular shape with the legs set centrally and the keel parallel to the ground does look rather unwieldy, however. Everything about a Rouen is large, long, broad and square. The bill is set in a straight line from the corner of the bold eye and the horizontal carriage accentuates the upright neck. The back slopes in a gentle curve down to the slightly raised tail, but the overall impression is of a rectangle. The drake goes into eclipse (duck coloured plumage) in the summer months, just like his ancestor the mallard, and young drakes do not get their adult plumage until they are about five months old. His bill is bright green-yellow with a black bean which contrasts nicely with the iridescent green head and neck. The white neck ring is incomplete at the back, and cleanly divides the neck and rich solid claret breast colour which continues down to the ground. The flank feathers are grey with glossy black fine pencilling, looking like chain mail, and this goes right up to the black tail with no white on the stern. The back is black and the grey wings must have a well-defined blue speculum with white bars. In both sexes the eyes are dark and the legs brick red.

　　The duck has a bright orange bill with a black saddle and a black bean. Her head is a rich golden brown striped with black and a strong dark stripe runs through the eye. The throat is slightly paler and the speculum is the same as in the drake with slate black primaries. The rest of the plumage has a ground colour of rich golden chestnut brown with every feather laced, double or triple, with black or dark brown. On a good specimen the markings are spectacular and even: they need to be as half the available show points are for colour in this breed. Eggs are white and fertility can be variable: the ducks have an infuriating habit of coming back into lay just

Rouen drake in full colour.

when the drake goes into eclipse and is less interested in mating. Ducklings need plenty of exercise as they grow and can be rather bossy, as can the adults, especially in a show pen – a clout with a Rouen wing on the hand gives judging an extra dimension – and the drakes particularly are good at hissing. Full size is really only gained after a year old, but mature birds live as long a life as other domestic ducks, despite their exaggerated size.

Faults to avoid include a roach back in either sex and fuzzy markings in the female.

Utility aspects
There are few extra eggs for eating and spare drakes take about six months to get any flesh. Some drake feathers are in demand for fishing flies.

Special requirements
Rouens need enough space to keep fit and a carefully regulated diet so that they grow to sufficient size.

Rouen ducks showing the important lacing.

SAXONY

Standard colours: one

This attractively coloured breed was developed in Germany between the wars and Standardised in 1982, having been imported into the UK in the 1970s. The creator wanted a fast-growing, dual purpose duck which was also beautiful and able to be exhibited.

Very popular due to the colouration, but getting the markings correct can be a challenge.

This is a comfortably large, strong breed with a slightly elevated carriage. The body is long and broad with a full breast and should have no trace of a keel. The legs are

Trio of young Saxony ducks.

Older Saxonies with the facing drake in full colour.

set just back from the midline and when the duck is in lay, her abdomen will be only just clear of the ground. The drake weighs 8lb (3.6kg) and the duck 7lb (3.2kg). The head and neck of the drake is a steel blue with no brown in it. The white neck ring is complete (other drakes to have this are the Silver Appleyard, page 56 and the Welsh Harlequin, page 61), but if there is a suspicion of a neck ring in the female, this is a fault. The breast is rusty red with some silver lacing and the back and rump is blue-grey with the lower body oatmeal. Wings are grey with a darker speculum. The duck is a most attractive deep apricot buff with white eyebrows and a white stripe from the eye to the bill. The throat is pale but should not extend into the breast colour. The speculum is pale grey and the flights are oatmeal. In both sexes the eyes are dark and the bills yellow with orange legs. Other faults to avoid are the drake breast colour running into the flanks, other than grey on the drake's head and white in the breast of the duck. As the birds get older, the bills can darken. The white egg production is good and the ducklings are strong and easy to rear, growing fast. This breed can become lazy and run to fat, especially the females, although in the breeding season the drake can lose weight quickly but still look large due to his profuse feathering – regular handling at this time will indicate when more food is needed.

Utility aspects
A true dual-purpose duck for both meat and eggs and with white down, the carcase plucks clean.

Special requirements
Care is needed to get the feeding correct so that the weight is maintained at a steady level, but this breed will cope in a fairly small area.

SILVER APPLEYARD

Standard colours: one. Large and miniature (⅓ size)

History
Reginald Appleyard created this duck between the wars as he wanted a fast-growing meat breed which laid well. Rather a tall order, but he certainly achieved his goal. Unfortunately, the colour had not really been stabilised and in the 1970s two colour types were available, both claiming to be the original. A painting by Wippell in 1947 was unearthed and these were pronounced the true type: they were subsequently Standardised after much work by dedicated breeders. The other type (without the drake head markings mainly) is still seen in farmyards, but cannot be exhibited unless in the AOV non-Standard class. The miniature version was created by Tom Bartlett in the 1970s and this follows the colour and type of the large, therefore very different from the Call ducks (page 22) and the Silver Bantam (page 59).

Current position
Popular not only for their speed of growth and production, but also their good looks. The miniature does not have the utility aspects, but is liked for its calm demeanour.

Pair of Silver Appleyard ducks.

Pair of miniature Silver Appleyard ducks.

Characteristics

This is an energetic and busy breed. The slightly erect carriage helps the mobility of the heavy but compact body which is broad and well rounded, allowing for plenty of meat. They should be chunky if not chubby. Weights are 8-9lb (3.6-4.1kg) in the drake and 7-8lb (3.2-3.6kg) in the duck. They reach this very quickly, at around 10 weeks, so are profitable to produce. There are plenty of white eggs which usually have high fertility and are easy to hatch with strong ducklings. The colour of the ducklings can vary slightly, so when selecting the breeding pens, do not be in too much of a hurry. The drake in adult plumage has a black-green head and neck with a silvery flecked throat and silvery eyebrows and cheek markings. The bill is yellow with a faint green tinge, but yellow should be selected for. A white ring completely encircles the neck (like the Saxony, page 54 and the Welsh Harlequin, page 61). The lower neck and breast is light claret and the breast feathers have a silver fringe on each one but the breast colour is split and the colour washes along the flanks, fading to silver on the abdomen. The scapulars are grey with a chestnut edge and the back is dark grey, going to black on the rump with white edging to the tail feathers. The flanks are light grey and the speculum must be iridescent blue, the wings being grey and white. The duck is basically silver-white with the top of the head and back of the neck fawn flecked with brown and this goes down to the shoulders and back without a break. There is a fawn stripe through the dark eye and the bill is yellow. The breast and underbody are creamy white, with fawn flecked with brown on the flanks and on the tail, plus the speculum must be iridescent blue with the wings creamy white. The bill is yellow but tends to have a brown saddle in order to keep the back colour right. Legs are orange in both sexes.

Miniatures should be smaller versions of the large, but are not kept for utility purposes although they lay quite well. They can fly well, so a wing may need to be clipped to keep them within bounds. They also have a light and a dark phase when breeding them – the more experienced breeders keep a few darks to use if the colour becomes too pale. The miniatures make excellent pets and become friendly quickly.

Utility aspects

The large Silver Appleyard is a good all-rounder with good meat and egg production.

Special requirements

Feeding must be carefully regulated due to the high rate of growth to avoid skeletal problems, but this breed is good for beginners. Watch that the drakes do not lose too much weight in the mating season. The miniature is a good breed for children.

SILVER BANTAM DUCK

Standard colours: one

History

This was originally called the Silver Appleyard bantam, as Appleyard himself created it, but when it was realised that the type and colour was different from the Standardised large version, a new title was chosen. In fact, this duck looks more like the Abacot Ranger (page 12). It was created as a broody duck for wildfowl, but has been muddled up both physically and in people's minds until a separate Standard was laid down.

Current position

Popular for hatching its own and other eggs, but not many are seen at the shows.

Characteristics

This is a small duck, the drake weighing 2lb (900g) and the duck 1¾lb (850g), but very active and a good forager. The drake has a green head and neck with a complete white ring dividing the green from the white-laced red-brown of the lower neck and breast. The belly, flank and stern are silver-white, the back grey leading to black on

Group of Silver Bantam ducks. The head colour of the females does vary.

the rump. The speculum is violet-green and the primaries white. The bill is yellow-green with a black bean and the eyes are dark plus orange legs in both sexes. The head of the duck is fawn with some graining of brown – she looks as though she has a sock on her head. The breast and shoulders are cream with brown streaks and the abdomen is cream. The rump is fawn-grey with brown flecking and the tail fawn. The speculum is also violet-green and the primaries white with the bill yellow to grey-green plus black markings on the saddle.

These birds make good pets as they are friendly and sensible. They will hatch either their own or other breed eggs sometimes twice in a season and make excellent mothers, shepherding their charges through the vegetation. As with the other silver types of duck, there are two colours that can appear from one hatch, the dark and the light, and it is better to run these on to an older age if you wish to exhibit so that the adult feathers can be seen at around twenty weeks. Remember to clip the primaries on one side to prevent the birds from flying off.

Utility aspects
There are clutches of eggs in the spring and summer, but the main use of the birds is for hatching out eggs. They are also good in the vegetable garden in the winter for slug and other insect control.

Special requirements
These birds are great foragers and fly well. They are very independent and will choose their own nest site whether safe from the fox or not, but are good for beginners and children.

WELSH HARLEQUIN

Standard colours: one

History

Harlequin by name and chequered by history, this breed nearly did not make it to modern times. The birds were first bred as sports from commercial Khaki Campbells by Group Captain Leslie Bonnet in the 1940s. The family then moved to Wales and these attractive birds were bred up to a flock, acquiring an equally attractive name in the process. They were, of course, excellent layers. In order to increase the carcase, Bonnet introduced Aylesbury and this cross (Whalesbury) was very popular locally. Unfortunately the pure flock was severely reduced by a fox and Bonnet was not able to reproduce the original sports. Some original Welsh Harlequins had been established in Lancashire in 1963, however, and these were bred back to Khakis by Eddie Grayson who then was so enthusiastic that he started the Welsh Harlequin Duck Club and achieved Standardisation of the breed in 1986. Stock was distributed all over the country and the controversy and confusion between the Welsh Harlequin, Whalesbury and Abacot Ranger (page 12) was resolved, at least on paper.

Current position

Plenty of stock is kept in the UK due to their production and attractiveness.

Two pairs of Welsh Harlequin, the drakes are not in full colour.

61

Due to their ancestry, this breed is in practice the same as the Khaki Campbell (page 26) in stance, production and shape, so they are slightly upright, alert and good foragers and the weights are the same – drakes 5-5$\frac{1}{2}$lb (2.25-2.5kg) and ducks 4$\frac{1}{2}$-5lb (2-2.25kg). The bill of the drake is olive-green without any trace of blue plus a black bean. The head and upper neck are iridescent green overlaid with bronze lustre. A sharply defined white ring completely encircles the neck (as in Saxony, page 54. and Silver Appleyard, page 56) and the breast, lower neck and shoulders are rich red-brown mahogany laced with white, the colour washing along the flanks, with the abdomen and stern creamy white. The scapulars and wing coverts are the same colour as the breast and due to the lacing have a rich tortoiseshell effect. The primaries are white overlaid with brown and the speculum must be bronze/green. The rump and undertail feathers are beetle-green, the tail is dark brown edged with white and the legs are dull orange. The duck has a gun-metal bill with a honey-fawn head plus brown graining on the crown. Her shoulders, breast, belly, flank and stern then fade through fawn to creamy white. Her back has a tortoiseshell pattern similar to the drake with white lacing on fawn and red-brown. The speculum must be bronze and the primaries are brown edged with white. The rump feathers are mid-brown with darker brown centres and the tail is mid-brown. The main faults to avoid are a wrong coloured speculum and yellow bill in the duck.

Welsh Harlequins are easy to breed, but not reliable as sitters, the eggs hatch well and the ducklings are strong. Like the Khakis, make sure the number of drakes is as low as possible, otherwise the ducks suffer severe feather shortage and trauma.

Utility aspects

Egg production is almost as good as the Khakis, but there is little flesh on spare drakes.

Special requirements

These need plenty of space for foraging and a low proportion of drakes. Egg numbers are improved if they are not let out until 9am – this avoids predation by magpies and crows.

Welsh Harlequin drake in full colour except for a few missing feathers on his throat.

Two Grey Chinese contrast with two Swan geese (Anser cygnoides) *which are the ancestors of both African and Chinese geese.*

AFRICAN

Standard colours: grey (brown), white, buff   *Ancestor:* swan goose

History

A French naturalist in 1793 described what we would recognise as an African goose, but called it a goose of Guinea. This is probably because anything new or strange at that time was generally termed 'guinea' or he may have thought it had travelled from the African Guinea coast. The African goose has retained its misnomer, however, despite the fact that similar geese have been known in China for centuries and are called 'Lion Head' – obvious from the photograph. Both the African and the Chinese geese (page 72) are descended from the wild swan goose (*Anser cygnoides*) rather than the greylag which is the ancestor of all the other domestic geese. The brown colour is identical, but the shape is vastly different. Some Africans were sent to America from China in Victorian times and this is where most of the modern UK stock comes from, but it was not until 1982 that the breed was Standardised. The Grey is the common colour, there are Buffs recently imported, but Whites have not been seen in the UK for several years.

Current position

Admired for their stateliness and character, there are fair numbers of the Grey African and they do well at the shows.

Characteristics

This is an extraordinary breed in character, looks and noise. They have a most distinctive, deep voice and are friendly and tame. They love going to the shows as they are usually the centre of attention especially as most of them can see out over the top of the 36in (91cm) show pens. The carriage is fairly upright, about 40° when alert. The head is broad, deep and large with the knob at the top of the upper mandible the same width as the head, pointing slightly forward. The dewlap is heavy and smooth with the lower edges regularly curved. It extends from the lower mandible to below the join of the neck and throat. The neck is broad and gracefully arched with velvety feathers (unlike the greylag descendants which have furrowed neck feathers) and the body is large and long with the topline and underline nearly parallel, the breast full and round without a keel. The tail is carried well up and the larger birds tend to have more of a paunch: it should not be too large, but symmetrical and dual lobed.

   The gander and goose are the same colour but it is confusing when the Grey is also known as the Brown or Fawn. The head is light brown with the neck light ashy brown (fawn) and a broad, dark brown stripe down the centre of the back of the neck to its full length. There is a faint brown line along the jaw and mature birds tend to have a narrow white line just behind the black knob with the black bill broad and stout at the base. The front of the neck changes from fawn to cream then back to fawn on the breast then paler on the abdomen to white on the stern. The flanks are ashy brown, each feather edged with a lighter shade, with stronger markings towards the tail which is ashy brown with white edging. The back is ashy brown with the wings dark slate and the covering feathers ashy brown with a light edge. The eyes

Pair of grey African geese.

are brown and the legs dark orange. Faults to avoid are white in the coloured plumage and lack of either the knob or the dewlap. Older birds sometimes have small amounts of orange in the knob due to wear and tear, however. The White is pure white with blue eyes and yellow bill and the Buff has the same pattern as the Grey but is buff with fawn on the lighter areas and a pinkish brown bill and knob.

Weights are 22-28lb (9.97-12.7kg) in the gander and 11-24lb (8.16-10.88kg) in the goose.

Africans make good parents, despite their large feet, but most breeders artificially incubate the eggs in order to get more stock. Do not let them sit for more than one clutch as they will lose too much condition. The goslings are delightful and cuddly when hand reared and also friendly when parent reared.

Utility aspects

Spare ganders are usually sold to other breeders, rather than eaten, and any large infertile eggs are in demand by artists for decoration.

Special requirements

Happy in fairly small areas, these geese nevertheless need lots of grass to graze. Be careful, by studying the characteristics, that they have not been crossed with Chinese.

AMERICAN BUFF

Standard colours: buff   *Ancestor:* greylag

History

With the greylag as ancestor and as the name implies, this breed was developed in America, but purely as a commercial goose and it seems there are no records of how it was bred. Not imported into the UK until 1980,when there was immediate confusion with the Brecon Buffs (page 69) and it took some time to unravel this.

Current position

In few hands today, but occasionally seen at the larger shows.

Characteristics

These are large, heavy meat birds and stand like Embdens (page 76). The ganders weigh 22-28lb (9.97-12.7kg) and the geese 20-26lb (9.07-11.79kg) and have an upright carriage with an upright long neck. The head is broad, oval and strong with a medium length stout bill and the body is moderately long and broad. The breast is full and the paunch should be symmetrical and dual lobed. The bill and legs must be orange, although some pink bills do appear occasionally. The feathers are a rich shade of buff throughout and the pattern is similar to the Toulouse (page 92) with white lacing on the back, shoulders and flanks and the stern, paunch and tail white with a broad band of buff across the tail. The neck feathers are furrowed. Faults to avoid include any white in the coloured plumage, although older birds may develop some white above the bill.

The birds are reasonably easy to breed and the goslings are strong and grow quickly. The geese are relatively good mothers, despite their size. In comparison with other breeds, the American Buff can appear coarse.

Utility aspects

Despite their weight, these geese do not have as high a meat to bone ration as, say, the Roman (page 85).

Special requirements

Before purchasing these, be very sure of the differences between them and the Brecon Buffs.

American Buff gander.

Pair of Brecon Buff with two goslings. The colour of the parents has faded in the sunlight.

BRECON BUFF

Standard colours: buff   *Ancestor:* greylag

History
Rhys Llewellyn of Swansea effectively started the first flock of Brecon Buffs by acquiring odd buff sports from commercial white flocks and breeding them together in the 1930s. When first exhibited against Embden (page 76) and Toulouse (page 92) in 1933 their attractiveness was proven and they were Standardised the following year.

Although smaller than the American Buff (page 66), the Brecon has a higher meat to bone ratio and was originally bred to be productive in harsh conditions on the Welsh hills. The attractive modern exhibition birds' characteristics have been strengthened, mostly due to the knowledge and enthusiasm of Welsh-living Chris and Mike Ashton, who also discovered that some geese feeding on the red sandstones of the Brecons had pink bills, but when moved to clay soils, the pink gave way to orange. With careful selection and breeding the essential pink colouration is more prevalent.

Current position
Buff is a popular colour and these neat geese will always have a strong following.

Characteristics
Smaller than the American Buff (page 66) but with more meat, the ganders weigh 16-20lb (7.25-9.07kg) and the geese 14-18lb (6.35-8.16kg). The carriage is upright and alert, indicating activity. The head is neat and the neck (with furrowed feathers) is medium length going smoothly into the round and full breast. The paunch is dual lobed and should be symmetrical. The bill and legs must be pink. The plumage is a deep shade of buff throughout with white lacing on the back, wings and flanks and the stern, paunch and tail are white with the tail having a broad band of buff across the centre. Ganders are usually a shade or two paler than the geese and the colour of both sexes tends to fade in sunlight, with the correct colour coming back again at the next moult. Older birds tend to have a small band of white around the bill and flecking on the lower breast feathers.

Brecons are reasonable layers and good at hatching their own, being very protective of their goslings where predators are concerned. Their temperament is mostly good, but aggression should be expected in the breeding season from established pairs. The goslings are a lovely caramel colour and if hand reared become very tame. They need extra feed, not just grass, if they are to get to table weight.

Utility aspects
Still useful as a meat breed with high meat to bone ratio, their maternal instincts and their hardiness plus exhibition potential makes these geese good all-rounders.

Special requirements
Try and obtain exhibition stock to get the correct colouring and characteristics. Brecons are good for beginners if sound stock is obtained.

Buff Back gosling.

BUFF BACK

Standard colours: buff and white (also Grey Back, *grey and white*)

Ancestor: greylag

History

Particoloured or pied geese have been known for centuries as they may be obtained by crossing whites with a solid colour and then breeding patterned to patterned to select for the desired coloured areas. See also Pomeranian (page 83).

Current position

Not a particularly popular breed.

Characteristics

Similar in style to the Embden (page 76) but smaller, these attractively coloured geese have a nearly horizontal carriage and look plump and meaty with no keel. The paunch is well developed and dual lobed. The head is slightly flat with a stout bill and large eyes and the neck is straight. The colour of the head and upper neck in the Buff Back is buff, the lower neck is white and on the back there is a heart-shaped buff area which has each feather laced with white. All else is white except for the flank feathers which are buff edged with white. In the Grey Back, the pattern is the same but the buff is replaced with grey. In both sexes the bills and legs are orange and the eyes blue. It can be challenging to get the markings in the correct place for exhibition purposes, but these geese are useful with weights in the adult ganders of 18-22lb (8.16-9.07kg) and the geese 16-20lb (7.25-9.07kg). The geese lay quite well and the goslings are strong and easy to rear.

There are other semi-coloured farmyard geese, some strains of which are sex-linked, where the gander is white and the geese have varying amounts of colour on them and some call these West of England. See also Pilgrim (page 80)

Utility aspects

Good for the table.

Special requirements

Care is needed with matching up the breeding birds to obtain the required coloured pattern.

CHINESE

Standard colours: white, grey (brown or fawn)   *Ancestor:* swan goose

History

Although known in China for centuries, these geese only came to the West after the 1780s, being recorded in America at that time. It seems there is no record of Chinese geese in Europe before the early 1800s and some were imported from China and America. The White was more popular to begin with as people were reminded of swans, but both colours were to be seen in St James's Park on the lake in the mid 1850s. The Victorians were more concerned with meat than eggs or ornament, so the birds were really only kept as commercial layers for crossing, until the Standard was approved in 1954 and classes laid on for them. These were the English variety which is larger and heavier in the neck than subsequent imports of American birds which are much more graceful and the Standards now reflect this later type. Both types are very noisy, excellent guards and can be of uncertain temper. Not only does a Chinese goose bite, it twists as it holds – excruciating.

Current position

There is plenty of stock in the UK, in both colours, of the American type, but the old fashioned English type (a better layer than the exhibition ones) is fast disappearing.

Characteristics

Graceful on both land and water, this upright goose has a long, slim, velvety, arched neck topped by a medium-sized head with a large, rounded, forward-pointing knob at the top of the bill. The gander's is larger than the goose's and does not reach full size until the bird is about two years old. The body is compact but looks plump with the breast carried high and forward. The paunch is well developed but there should be a smooth underline with no lobes and the plumage is tight and sleek. The tail is carried high with the wings crossing over just above it and the bold eye enhances the impression of an alert and active bird. The colours are the same in both sexes: the White is pure white with bill and knob orange, plus legs orange-yellow and blue eyes. The Grey has the same colouring as the Grey African and is also confusingly known as Brown or Fawn Chinese: with the three colours in the bird, the three names seem interchangeable. The knob and bill in the Grey are black (avoid orange) and in mature specimens there is a narrow band of white feathers behind this. A bold dark brown stripe goes from the crown through the dark eye and all the way down the back of the neck with a faint shadow on the lower jawline. The lower head is fawn, shading to cream on the throat, then back to fawn on the lower neck and breast, becoming white on the stern. The flanks are ashy brown with near-white edging, as are the scapulars, with the back ashy brown. The primaries are dark slate with the tail ashy brown with white edging and the legs are dull orange. Weights are 10-12lb (4.55-5.45kg) in the gander and 8-10lb (3.6-4.55kg) in the goose, making them the smallest and lightest of the domestic geese. Avoid white in the coloured

Pair of White Chinese.

Pair of Grey Chinese.

areas of the Grey as this usually indicates crossing with the White, any sign of a gullet and a gander with a small knob.

Egg production has been known to top 80 in a year, but most Chinese lay around 30 eggs, not all in the same clutch. They are unreliable sitters and most eggs are artificially incubated or put under other geese or broody ducks or hens. The eggs are quite small, so not really in demand by egg decorators, but spare eggs are good for baking. Hand reared goslings can be a nuisance if they imprint only on humans and while it is good to get them tame when they are young, they need company of their own kind, or at least other waterfowl. Adults are alert and good guards, but they bicker amongst themselves, giving them a noisy reputation.

Utility aspects

Egg production is higher than other geese and they can lay at other times in the year than spring. However, the carcase is small. Guarding comes naturally to them.

Special requirements

They look so good on water and love swimming so much that a pond is greatly appreciated. Be careful that small children do not get entangled with an angry Chinese goose or gander as they can do some damage.

EMBDEN

Standard colours: white   *Ancestor:* greylag

History

There have been different types of big white meat geese in the UK and Northern Europe for centuries. The UK stock was broader and chunkier and the German stock was slimmer necked with a finer head. Some German stock was exported to America, so the differences in the types have been maintained. Recently, with the UK massive exhibition stock becoming increasingly difficult to breed, German examples have been introduced to increase fertility and egg production. The exchange of stock has meant that the two types are beginning to merge, making it less easy for judges and breeders alike. Also, Toulouse has been used on the English Embdens which, while increasing egg production, gave the legacy of unwanted dewlaps and keels.

Current position

There has been a slight increase of show entries in recent years, but numbers are still low.

Characteristics

Everything about this goose is massive: it stands at least 3 feet (about a metre) tall. The head is deep, strong and bold with a bill which is stout at the base. The blue eyes are bold and the long neck (without a gullet) has the typical furrowed feathers of the greylag (German birds tend to have less furrowing and a much finer head and neck). The stance is upright and the broad body is thick and well rounded with top and underline parallel until the large dual lobes come down between the strong legs. The glossy white plumage is tight and hard and the bill and legs are orange. The weights are 28-34lb (12.7-15.4kg) for the gander and 24-28lb (10.8-12.7kg) for the goose. The shape of the body and the size carry the most points in exhibiting: it is too easy to lose the size in subsequent generations, so careful feeding and husbandry is needed to maximise growth rates, but the best goslings grow at such a phenomenal rate that feeding of protein, particularly, has to be curtailed to avoid gout. The eggs are also huge: infertile ones much in demand by the egg decorators. They are nowadays much more fertile and easier to hatch than they used to be a few years ago. The goslings can still vary in size and need lots of exercise so that their large feet and legs remain strong enough for the adult weights and a rough surface just after they hatch is essential for their legs to remain straight. Egg numbers reach about thirty in a season, but they do start to lay in February, which is earlier than most other geese, and the females like to go broody, but they can be very clumsy with the goslings.

Avoid birds with a dewlap or keel or any colour in the plumage.

Utility aspects

Bred originally for meat, spare ganders can also be used as crosses on better egg laying breeds to produce a good carcase.

Pair of breeding Embden geese showing the heavy abdomen of the female.

Embden gander at an exhibition.

Greylag goose (Anser anser), *the ancestor of all domestic geese except African and Chinese.*

Special requirements

Experience is needed in feeding and management so that nutritional levels are correct to ensure maximum growth with strong bones. Not a breed for the beginner.

Embdens are all white but by no means are all white geese Embdens.

PILGRIM

Standard colours: the ganders are all white and the geese are grey

Ancestor: greylag

History

The legend has it that these were the geese that accompanied the Pilgrim Fathers on the *Mayflower* and thus obtained their name, which is a nice story but unfortunately only partially true. The local grey and white farmyard geese would have been taken to America at that time, as were other types of poultry, but the geese were not christened 'Pilgrim' until Oscar Grow developed his strain in the 1930s, and then only due to his own family's pilgrimage across America. All farmyard geese developed from the greylag have for centuries been a mixture of white and grey. Some people then selected for the ganders being mostly white and the geese mostly grey (the West of England, see page 94, is like this grey and white farmyard strain). Some of these strains were also auto-sexing or sex-linked, i.e. one sex was always the same colour but different from the other sex colour. It was not until the 1980s that Pilgrims were exhibited and then, subsequently, stock was imported from Canada.

Current position

In the hands of very few breeders, these attractive geese are difficult to get correctly marked.

Characteristics

Standing slightly upright, the Pilgrim is a medium sized bird with ganders 14-18lb (6.35-8.16kg) and geese 12-16lb (5.44-7.25kg). The head is medium sized and oval with a medium bill which is straight. The body is moderately long and plump with a deep abdomen plus dual lobes but these should be symmetrical and not baggy. The gander should be all white but some grey is allowed on the back, especially in young birds. His bill and legs are orange and his eyes are blue. The goose is mostly grey. Her bill is orange and her eyes brown and there is a little white on the head, a spectacle pattern around the eyes being the most common. The white on the head tends to increase with age but should not go down the neck or be on the breast. The rest of the head and the neck is light grey and the back is light ashy grey laced with lighter grey. The breast is light ashy grey fading to near-white at the stern, the flanks are ashy grey, each feather edged with a lighter shade and the wings are grey. The tail is grey but heavily edged with near-white. Avoid females that have white on the breast and white primaries.

The geese lay quite well and make good mothers if allowed to sit. They are not easy to artificially incubate and the goslings can come out slightly different colours even from a good set of parents. There may also be the odd white female and males with too much grey: few strains are completely auto-sexing. Geese are easy to sex before 4 weeks of age (page 118), but for those who do not wish to learn how to do this, an auto-sexing breed may be the answer, even though it is not 100%. The other problem is how do you know a white gander is a Pilgrim? The answer is you cannot just by looking at him: it is only when he has been bred to a pure female and produced the correct progeny that he may be declared pure. The breed is fraught with difficulty and is not for beginners.

Pair of Pilgrim, the gander is behind the goose.

Utility aspects

Certainly good for the table and there are a reasonable number of eggs to allow some spare, but most exhibitors set every egg.

Special requirements

Careful culling is necessary to obtain the correct markings. Do not be misled by being told some grey and white geese are Pilgrim without further research into their ancestry.

Pomeranian gander at an exhibition.

POMERANIAN

Standard colours: grey and white saddleback, solid grey, solid white

Ancestor: greylag

History

Geese were documented as being an important agricultural product of the marshy areas of Germany in 1550. They probably followed the pattern of being derived from an Embden/Toulouse cross, and the distinctive saddleback pattern is found in other parts of the world. However, the Pomeranian is the only goose of this type to have a single lobe, Standardised in Germany in 1929. The first Pomeranians were imported into the UK in the early 1980s from America and then, when compared to the German Standard, selection was able to be made.

Current position

There are a few breeders of this useful goose and classes at the larger shows are reasonably well attended.

Characteristics

The nearly horizontal carriage makes this goose look plump and meaty and the stout neck is carried upright, having an even width. The head has a slightly flat crown, giving the goose a haughty and confident look and the stout bill is straight and the eyes prominent. The back is slightly rounded with the wings carried closely folded and there is a single, central lobe between the legs. The colour is the same in goose and gander with solid dark grey on the head and upper neck where the furrowing of the feathers is easily seen. Some older birds have a small amount of white behind the bill, but the less of this, the better. The lower neck, breast, wings, tail and stern are white. The back is dark grey edged with grey-white, forming a heart-shape from the shoulders down to the tail. The flanks are dark grey edged with grey-white and in some birds there is a dark grey band joining the flanks under the abdomen. The bill in both sexes is reddish pink and the legs are orange red with the eyes blue. The ganders are 18-24lb (8.2-10.9kg) and the geese 16-20lb (7.3-9.1kg). The birds are dual purpose and lay well, producing over 35 eggs in a season which can extend later than other breeds. The eggs can be large, which the egg decorators like, and the goslings hatch reasonably easily and are strong. The coloured pattern can be seen at dayold, so any culls may be done then, or surplus birds grown on for meat. It can be frustrating to breed these birds as a really good bird may have one side correct for markings and the other side is not symmetrical. The geese make good, quiet mothers and the ganders understandably get protective in the breeding season.

Avoid dual lobes or a single lobe which is off-centre and any badly mismarked birds.

In Germany, there is also a solid grey Pomeranian and a solid white one.

Utility aspects

These are truly dual purpose geese.

Group of Pomeranians.

Special requirements

These need plenty of grass and fresh water, but are otherwise undemanding. Good for beginners who wish to exhibit and use the culls for meat.

ROMAN

Standard colours: white   *Ancestor:* greylag

History

These are the sacred geese which alerted the Romans to the attack of the Gauls on the Capitol and thus saved Rome in 5BC. It is well known that geese make good guards for their own flock and its territory as a survival instinct and this is due to the facts that firstly, they set scouts, and secondly, all waterfowl can sleep with one half of the brain and one eye at a time (as can dolphins), so alertness is maintained. Small white geese have been known in Europe for centuries and when the Romans arrived in Britain, they found that the natives also kept sacred geese. The small geese in Europe were generally known as Italian geese and imported into the UK in 1903.

Roman goose.

Seen at shows in smaller numbers than in the 1990s, but breeders are dedicated to these diminutive birds.

Characteristics

The carriage is almost horizontal, but these birds give the appearance of alertness and activity. The fine head is well rounded with a deep face and short bill and the piercing blue eyes set high. The neck is short which makes it look thick, but particularly in the goose should be refined, with the usual furrowing of the feathers. The body is plump, deep and broad with a full breast. There is no keel. The paunch should not be too pronounced – this tends to happen in older geese which have been good breeders – and is dual lobed. The tail is quite long, as are the wings which are carried high up. The all-white plumage is sleek, tight and glossy and the bill and legs are orange-pink. These are probably the most economical geese for meat production as they grow very fast and also lay well. They are supposed to have the highest meat to bone ratio of all the geese and at 12-14lb (5.45-6.35kg) for ganders and 10-12lb (4.55-5.45kg) for geese, they make a very respectable carcase. They are small, neat geese and do well in confined areas, as long as they have plenty of grass. The geese will hatch their own or other goose eggs and make good parents, being very protective. They have a nasty twisty bite which sees off most intruders, but seem docile with their owners.

The eggs (up to 30 in a season) are quite small, but hatch well and the goslings are strong. The best exhibition strains, as in all poultry, are not as productive, however. Avoid overly large birds with a keel or a long neck.

There is a tufted version (not large enough to be called a crest) in America and, as in all geese, the tuft is just a few raised feathers on the crown of the head. Tufted individuals in any breed of goose may be found occasionally.

Utility aspects

Mainly used for meat, these lay well and are good mothers.

Special requirements

All small white geese are not proper Romans – beware of buying just any old stock which happens to be called by the same name. These feisty geese do well in confined spaces but need plenty of grass.

SEBASTOPOL

Standard colours: white in frizzled and smooth-breasted types, also buff

Ancestor: greylag

History

Small white geese have been common in Europe for centuries. These rather untidy-looking loose and long-feathered birds appear to have originated around the Danube area and were known by this name for a while. Once imported into the UK in the 1850s, they were known as Sebastopols, possibly as this was the port of departure. Their extraordinary feather structure, or lack of it, was a talking point in Victorian times but, although they look ornamental, they have reasonable utility features.

Current position

Kept both for ornament and some utility, these interesting geese have a strong following.

Characteristics

The horizontal carriage and the fluffy feathers make the Sebastopol look like a round ball with an upright neck. The head is neat and fine with a medium bill and large eyes.

Sebastopol geese swimming with their family.

The feathers of the back, shoulders, wings and tail are long, curled and trailing, almost to the ground. In the frizzled, the breast feathers are curled as well, but the smooth-breasted has normal feathers. The head and neck feathers are smooth in both types, with the usual furrowing. The smooth-breasted has longer trailing feathers than the frizzle and these obscure the legs. If birds are to be exhibited, they need to be kept in very clean conditions as the feathers, once stained, are almost impossible to clean up and the feather condition carries the most points. The White is all white, although the youngsters have some grey feathers on the back which moult out, and the Buff is an even colour. Eyes are blue in the White and brown in the Buff and legs and bills are orange in both colours. The ganders are 12-16lb (5.44-7.25kg) and the geese 10-14lb (4.53-6.35kg).

Angel wing is more of a problem in this breed than some others, probably due in part to the feather structure, so be careful of the protein levels in the young birds. Avoid birds with lack of the frizzled or trailing feathers and a keel.

Sebastopols lay well and make good parents. The goslings are strong and easy to rear. There is also enough meat on spare ganders to be useful.

Utility aspects

Reasonably easy to breed, these geese have plenty of eggs and make a reasonable carcase.

Special requirements

If the birds are to be used for exhibition, an area free of mud is essential. Apart from a tendency towards angel wing, these are relatively trouble-free birds, but look too scruffy for some people.

Pair of Sebastopol geese with four goslings, the two paler ones are older and were adopted.

STEINBACHER

Standard colours: blue   *Ancestor:* greylag and swan goose

History

Unique among Standardised domestic geese for its dual ancestry, the Steinbacher was developed in what was East Germany around 1900. The local geese of greylag ancestry were crossed with the Asiatics (Chinese and African geese) to make strong fighting geese. This breed began in grey and then its distinctive blue colour was Standardised in 1951. Blue in geese is rare and in other types of poultry is not a fixed colour, but this goose breeds a true colour which is fixed, possibly with the help of the Asiatic genes. Not only the colour is distinctive – the stance and the shape of the head and bill is unlike any other geese. These were only imported into the UK in the late 1980s but were immediately liked.

Current position

Although the numbers are not large in the UK, the breed is popular for its colour and attitude.

Characteristics

Although bred in the same way as fighting geese, Steinbachers are sensible, calm and confident with people. In the breeding season, however, they must be kept separate from other breeds, including not being able to reach through wide netting, as they are very tenacious and can do some damage to less aggressive breeds. The whole stance of the bird is confident and arrogant as it holds its head and bill slightly elevated. The impression of a Roman nose adds to this as the straight bill is set in a straight line with the skull. The black serrations on the orange bill and the black bean are important to maintain as a breed characteristic. The neck is straight with feather furrowing and the medium-sized body gives the impression of stockiness. A smooth underline with no paunch is preferred in young stock, but older birds can acquire a small dual lobed paunch. The wings are carried tightly, but do not cross above the tail. The head, neck, breast, back, wings and thighs are light blue-grey, sometimes called lavender in other breeds. The neck has a faint very slightly darker blue stripe down the back of it. The shoulder, wing and thigh feathers are laced with white and the tail is grey with white lacing. The abdomen, stern and back are silver-blue. The eyes are brown and the legs orange. The ganders are 13-15lb (6-7kg) and the geese 11-13lb (5-6kg) but they do not lay at all well, one clutch is often all that is produced. The eggs are not difficult to hatch, but fertility seems to be a problem, hence these birds are scarce.

    Avoid birds with a knob, a dewlap, a keel or a strong stripe down the back of the neck. Other colours are Standardised in Europe and include Buff, Cream and Grey.

Utility aspects

Unless mismarked birds are used for the table, this is more of an ornamental breed.

Pair of Steinbacher. These are relaxed: the gander usually has his bill arrogantly pointing upwards.

Special requirements

Separate accommodation is needed in the breeding season and careful egg collection is advised due to the low numbers laid. A lovely breed to keep, even for beginners, but they are not productive and obtaining replacement stock is not easy.

TOULOUSE

Standard colours: grey, buff, white   *Ancestor:*greylag

History

The Earl of Derby brought some grey geese from France to England in the 1840s. These were larger than any geese seen before, but they did not look like the modern exhibition Toulouse. This part of France is where *pâté de foie gras* was invented. The larger grey geese were grown on until adult and then put in a small coop and force fed so that the liver enlarged after a few weeks and then they were killed. Considered a delicacy and a luxury, *pâté* is not usually now eaten by people who know how it is produced. The birds had a large abdomen in order to accommodate the enlarged liver and this exaggeration has been developed in the exhibition birds. They proved popular with the Victorians, but it was not until the divergent lines of birds in the UK and America were mixed in the 1970s that the modern exhibition bird had a better chance of reaching its peak. The exhibition Toulouse (or Giant Dewlap) is a much more exaggerated creature. Toulouse are large grey geese but not all large grey geese are Toulouse. Beware of buying birds called Toulouse unless the parents have been seen. The young stock takes months if not years to mature fully and unscrupulous breeders will sell off sub-standard stock saying they will get better when they get older. A good Toulouse will look good as a gosling – all the bits such as keel and dewlap will be showing, just not fully developed.

Current position

Good exhibition birds are in the hands of few breeders. Newcomers tend to give up on them when they realise the time and difficulty involved in breeding these huge birds, but the utility Toulouse are popular and breed more easily.

Characteristics

The exhibition birds are oblong in body shape with nearly horizontal carriage: these stately birds seem to glide slowly along the ground. The massive head has a strong, straight, short bill and the dewlap begins at the base of the bill and extends in folds down the upper neck. There are also loose cheek folds which enhance the size of the head and the neck is long and thick with the furrowed feathers prominent. The back is slightly curved from the neck to the tail and the breast is deep and full with the keel a straight line to the stern in relaxed birds. From the front, the keel can be seen to be supported by muscular bands reaching the ribs and the paunch and stern are full, wide and heavy with a rising sweep to the tail. The legs are set centrally to support the weight which is 26-30lb (11.79-13.6kg) in the gander and 20-24lb (9.07-10.88kg) in the goose. Plumage is rather soft and the Grey has the head and neck grey with the breast and keel lighter in colour. The flanks are darker and the back, wings and flanks are grey with each feather laced with an almost white edging. The wings are grey and the stern, paunch and tail are white, the tail having a broad band of grey across the centre. The bill is orange in both sexes and the legs are deep reddish orange. The eyes are dark, as they are in the Buff, and the Buff is identical in shape to the Grey but has buff replacing the grey. The White has blue eyes and is pure white, but with the same shape as the Grey. There are very few Buff or White Toulouse available in the UK.

Pair of Toulouse. The gander (sideways on) is nervous and has hitched up his keel.

Breeding is rather hit and miss as fertility declines with age – a Toulouse is old at ten years, whereas other breeds go on sometimes twice as long – and if the goose goes broody, that usually puts paid to any more eggs in that season. Do not let her sit as she will lose condition very fast and may never really get back to her full size. Fertile eggs hatch well, but the goslings are quiet and rather timid and may get pushed off the food by other breeds. They need lots of exercise, rather like Rouens (page 51) in order to grow and remain fit. There is a tendency for angel wing and dropped tongue to be a problem in some strains.

Utility birds are much easier to breed and rear, but they do not have the classic lines of the exhibition birds, being more upright and much less exaggerated. There is no Standard for the utility birds.

Utility aspects

If exhibition birds, none, except a bit of grass control. If utility type, then both eggs and meat are useful.

Special requirements

Space to grow at their own pace is needed and some pairs can be less enthusiastic about mating until they are put with other mates – sometimes they have to choose their own, rather like Call ducks (page 22). If exhibition birds are wanted, visit the breeders before buying to see the quality of stock.

WEST OF ENGLAND

This is the typical farmyard goose with the ganders nearly all white and the geese white and grey, preferably with symmetrical markings. It is larger than the Pilgrim (page 80) and some strains are auto-sexing.

The **Shetland** is a smaller version of the West of England.

TURKEYS

Group of turkey stags: Buff, Bourbon Red, Pied, American Wild and Slate.

TURKEYS

Standard colours: bourbon red, British white, bronze, buff, Cambridge bronze, crimson dawn or black winged bronze, cröllwitzer (pied), Norfolk black, slate.
Other colours not yet Standardised in UK: Narragansett, Royal Palm, Ronquières, lavender, Nebraskan spotted.

Ancestor: Meleagris gallopavo gallopavo (Mexico) and *Meleagris gallopavo silvestris* (eastern seaboard of North America)

History

The turkey was first domesticated in Mexico by the Aztec Indians as early as AD1000 and the first arrival in Europe of these birds was in 1524. The origin of the name is shrouded in different theories, but the Aztec name for them is *toto*, some place names in Mexico still containing this. They were brought into Britain by William Strickland of Yorkshire and would have been the Mexican race which is bronze with white in its tail feathers. The *M.g. silvestris* is also bronze but has chestnut instead of the white and once these were imported to the UK in the 1700s, the various other colours were developed, including the buff series. Documentation of sports of other colours, even from earliest times, has been found. There are other subspecies of turkey in North America, but it was not until the domesticated version was brought back to the USA that the huge turkey meat industry was started and some of those birds were crossed back to the wild ones, creating more colours. The first turkeys to be exhibited in the UK were in 1845, with a Standard appearing in the first *Book of Standards* in 1865. Ronquières is a small type of turkey in Belgium and comes in a variety of colours.

Current position

Turkeys are enjoying a revival in numbers due to their personalities and choice of colours, ease of production and suitability for organic systems. A Turkey Club has recently been formed and has an enthusiastic following. It is the dedicated breeders who exhibit, however, as these large birds take some transporting.

Characteristics

It must be remembered that commercial turkeys are very much heavier and meatier than the 'pure breed' ones, the broad breasted bronze record being 96lb (43.5kg)! These birds are obviously too large to mate properly and in the industry, artificial insemination is practised almost without exception. The white is of course favoured over the bronze as it plucks clean, but recently a smaller commercial bronze has been developed for free-range enterprises. Thus the pure breeds are long-lived, slim, coloured, active and hardy birds, but the range of weights is from a fine 18lb (8.6kg) in the young Blue stag to a sturdy 40lb (18.1kg) in the mature Bronze stag. Although these birds are weighty, the meat is more evenly distributed, rather than being mostly on the breast like the commercial ones. These are known as 'high breasted' as opposed to broad breasted and as such are more likely to be run free-range, therefore giving a better flavour carcase. The stags and sometimes older hens, develop a tassel which is composed of thick, coarse, hair-like feathers growing in a bunch from the top of the breast. This increases in length with the age of the bird.

The head should be long, broad and carunculated with an extensible snood in the centre of the forehead, much larger in the stags. The beak is strong and curved and the eyes are bold and prominent. The throat wattle is large and pendant, but larger in the stag. The hens have sparse feathers on top of their heads and the colour of the bare skin can range from white to red to blue, depending on mood. The body is long, deep and well-rounded with strong and large wings and a long tail containing 18 feathers. The legs are stout and strong with long claws on the toes. When displaying, the stags hold their necks towards their upright tails with their breasts puffed out and make a 'poomph' noise by displacing air. Sometimes a hen will display if agitated and it is amusing to see toy-like poults practising their display technique.

Individual colours are described below as turkeys are basically all the same breed with the same characteristics.

It is usual to have a turkey stag with two or three hens in the breeding pen. Stags are rather slow at mating and spend a long time treading (literally) on the backs of the hens. This can lead not only to feather damage but can split the flanks of the hens severely. It is best to fit the hens with a leather or strong cloth 'saddle' in the breeding season. These are obtainable from various sources advertising in the poultry press and the saddle is shaped like an apple with a loop of material on each 'shoulder' which goes around the wings, the bulk of the material protecting the back and flanks of the hen.

Turkeys are insatiably curious and will get into all sorts of mischief. Their large eyes mean they miss nothing going on around them and they are expert at catching insects and eating weeds – docks do not have a chance in a turkey pen, but neither do flowers as turkeys will eat almost any plant. Their boredom threshold is low and if there is nothing else to do, they will pick on one of their own number and have a mugging session. They are very vocal – a poult stuck somewhere will shout 'weepe, weepe' for hours – and the stags will always answer you if you call to them or imitate the noise of the hens, a 'keow, keow' being the most successful, and the alarm call is a 'putt, putt'. Small children love the noise competition!

The hens fly well, particularly when looking for a nesting site, so a clipped wing (page 117) is useful here. Young stags can fly a bit, but they get more sedentary as they get heavier. However, a three foot (one metre) high fence is easily jumped/ flapped onto by stags of any age. All turkeys love to perch at night when roosting and if not given a perch will get up onto inappropriate heights such as roofs. Their flock instinct is powerful, which makes them good guards in daylight, but they do not see well in the dark, unlike waterfowl. This flocking makes them easy to move by driving if done slowly.

All turkeys are immensely strong which makes handling quite difficult. Use a strong fishing landing net to catch them or drive them into a corner, but beware they do not fly onto something unreachable. Unless the wings are restrained when carrying them, a nasty thick lip can ensue, but they rarely bite. When fighting each other, they lock on with their beaks and use their strong legs and claws. If a stag decides that he dislikes a person or just people generally, he can be dangerous as he kicks out and clouts with his wings. A solution involving the cooking pot is really the only answer as turkeys have but one idea in their heads at a time and it is difficult to change this. They have higher blood pressure than other poultry, so be careful when catching them. If transporting them any distance, be aware that their droppings are

Turkey poults enjoy catching insects and eating grass.

particularly pungent. Turkeys live for about 10 years and generally improve in size with age, but the weight of the stags as they get older may need adjusting.

The eggs are larger than chicken eggs, shaped similarly with a broad end but with a distinct pointed end. The shells are white or cream coloured and have varying amounts of brown speckling and spotting on them (see page 113). As in chickens, the eggs increase in size as the birds get older and they are good to eat boiled, having a texture the same as a chicken egg, and, being larger, go further in cooking. Hens will lay between 50 and 100 eggs a year, mostly between March and July. The eggs take 28 days to hatch and turkey hens make good mothers if allowed to sit. Most breeders use a 'sin-bin' (coop with wire floor, no perch, plus food and water) to de-broodify the birds for 14 days as otherwise they lose condition and the number of eggs is reduced.

Dayold turkeys are very cuddly and love human company. They are not difficult to rear as long as proper turkey food is used as this contains the correct level of protein and drugs to inhibit the killer parasite, blackhead. (See Appendices 3 & 4 for further management and health information.) They love playing games and sparring as they get older, and they need shade in hot weather. Sexing is not easy until the stags begin to grow away from the hens, becoming larger at about 12 weeks. The hens retain feathers on their heads for longer and the earliest they can lay is 30 weeks, but normally it is the following spring after hatching. If young stags are to be kept together for meat production, it is sometimes useful to put an older stag in with them to keep the peace. Turkeys can be killed at any time from 22 weeks for meat, as long as there is a bloom of fat under the skin and the feathers are through a moult.

Utility aspects

An all-rounder as there are a good number of eggs, meat production is fairly fast, the hens will brood and weed control is useful if organised properly.

Special requirements

Turkeys do need lots of space and vegetation. They can be kept with other poultry as long as they are all wormed regularly, but beware of aggressive and hooligan tendencies.

PLUMAGE COLOURS

Standard
Bourbon Red

The stag's head and neck are brownish-red. The rest of the body is rich, dark, brownish-red, each feather with a narrow black edging. The wings are white and the tail is white with an indistinct red bar. The hen is the same colour as the stag but with no black edging to the feathers and narrow white edging on the breast feathers. The eyes are brown with horn-coloured beak and legs. The poults are brownish. Weights are 22-28lb (9.97-12.7kg) for a mature stag and 12-18lb (5.44-8.16kg) for a mature hen. Only a few are in the UK.

Classification: Light

Bourbon Red turkey trio sunbathing.

British White

The plumage is pure white in both sexes with a black tassel. Eyes are dark blue with a white beak and pink legs. Weights are 28lb but not exceeding 38lb (12.7-17.23kg) in the mature stag and 16-22lb (7.25-9.97kg) in the mature hen. Rarely seen at shows, but the commercial bird is white and much heavier. The poults are pure white.

Classification: Heavy.

Bronze

The body feathers are black with a broad metallic bronze band, giving the overall effect of solid metallic bronze. The hen has fine white banding on her breast. The primaries are black with distinct white barring and the secondaries are less sharply marked. The tail feathers are black with brown barring, ending in a broad bronze band followed by a broad white band, each change of colour to be as distinct as possible. The eyes are dark, the beak horn and the legs dark. The poults are brown and dark brown striped. Weights are 30-40lb (13.6-18.14kg) in the mature stag and 18-26lb (8.16-11.79kg) in the mature hen. Probably the most popular and numerous colour, certainly the most well known.

Classification: Heavy.

Two Bronze stags displaying to each other: the snoods can be seen dangling down over the beaks.

(LEFT) *British White hen in ready to fly pose.*

Two Bronze hens with the evening sun on their backs, enhancing the bronze colouration.

Buff hen with a black turkey chick, one of a group of different coloured turkey poults being reared.

Buff

Cinnamon-brown is the colour of these throughout the body of both sexes and there is no black banding anywhere or white on the breast of the hen. The primaries and secondaries are white and the tail is deep cinnamon-brown edged with white. The eyes are dark and the legs pink. The poults are pale brown. Weights are 22-28lb (9.97-12.7kg) in the mature stag and 12-18lb (5.44-8.16kg) in the mature hen. There are few good examples of Buff.

Classification: Light.

The head of a Buff stag showing the snood mostly retracted. The tassel is long on this 4-year-old bird.

Cambridge Bronze

This is a dull bronze with grey and white tips to the body feathers and barred wings and tail as in the Bronze. The eyes and legs are dark and the weights are 5lb (2.3kg) less than the Bronze. Nowhere near as popular as the Bronze and closer to the commercial bronze colouring.

Classification: Heavy.

Crimson Dawn or Black Winged Bronze

This is a black winged version of the Bronze but should have a crimson tinge to the feathers. Very few are seen.

Classification: Heavy.

Cröllwitzer

This used to be known as Pied and the Royal Palm in the USA is similar – it is a good judge who can tell the subtle differences between them. The neck is white and the body feathers are white with a black band edged with white throughout, the black tending to become broader towards the tail. The primaries are white with a black edge and the tail is white with a distinct black band followed by white at the edge. The eyes are brown and the legs horn-coloured. The poults are white, the black markings appearing as they get older. Weights are 16-28lb (7.25-12.7kg) in the mature stag and 8-18lb (3.62-8.16kg) in the mature hen. This is a popular colour but getting the markings free of mossiness can be challenging.

Classification: Light.

Cröllwitzer or Pied stag displaying.

Norfolk Black hen.

Norfolk Black

These should be a dense, glossy black throughout. There should be no white anywhere and most specimens have slight bronze bands in the tail – the less of this, the better. The eyes and legs are dark and the poults are black with a white face and some white on the underside. Weights are 25lb (11.35kg) in the mature stag and 13-15lb (5.9-6.8kg) in the mature hen. Plenty of turkeys called Norfolk Black are available, but good, solid black ones are difficult to find.

Classification: Light.

Slate

Getting the slaty blue an even shade throughout is challenging as brown tends to creep in, especially in the tail. The blue can be a dark or light shade as long as it is even, but darker birds are preferred at the shows. Some strains tend to black spots in the feathers, but the less of this, the better. The eyes are dark and the legs slate. The poults are pale grey. Weights are 18-25lb (8.16-11.33kg) in the mature stag and 14-18lb (6.35-8.16kg) in the mature hen. This is a popular colour but there are few breeders.

Classification: Light.

Narragansett

This is Standardised in the USA and is patterned like the Bronze. The body colour is steel grey with a narrow black band on each feather, becoming solid glossy black on the back, then each feather banded with steel grey above the tail. The primaries and secondaries are distinctly barred with black and white and the tail is black barred with tan, ending in a black band edged with a broad band of pale steel grey. There should be no bronze cast in the black. Weights are 30lb (13.6kg) in the stag and 18lb (8.16kg) in the hen.

Pair of Narragansett turkeys. They have the same pattern as the Bronze, but bronze is replaced by steel grey. In the tail of the hen can be seen new feathers growing through with undamaged border markings.

(LEFT) *Slate stag displaying. This chap lost part of his snood in a fight.*

Lavender

This colour is not yet Standardised, but should be a pale, even shade of blue throughout with no brown or black. Popular, but not easy to obtain. Weights as in the Slate.

Nebraskan Spotted

This colour is also not yet Standardised. The basic body colour is white with irregular red and black flecks or spots with white wings and tail and an indistinct cream band near the edge of it. The poults are cream and gradually acquire the other colours as they get older. Weights as in the Slate.

Two Lavender turkey hens. Ideally, they should be a solid lavender colour with no lacing.

(RIGHT) *Pair of Nebraskan Spotted turkeys.*

Appendix 1
COMPLETE CLASSIFICATION OF BREEDS

DUCKS

Heavy	Light	Bantam
Aylesbury	Abacot Ranger	Black East Indian
Blue Swedish	Bali	Call
Cayuga	Campbell	Crested
Muscovy	Crested	Silver Appleyard Miniature
Pekin	Hook Bill	Silver Bantam
Rouen Clair	Indian Runner	
Rouen	Magpie	
Saxony	Buff Orpington	
Silver Appleyard	Welsh Harlequin	

GEESE

Heavy	Medium	Light
African	American Buff	Chinese
Embden	Brecon Buff	Pilgrim
Toulouse	Buff Back	Roman
	Grey Back	Sebastopol
	Pomeranian	Steinbacher

TURKEYS

Heavy	Light
British White	Bourbon Red
Bronze	Buff
Cambridge Bronze	Cröllwitzer (Pied)
Crimson Dawn	Norfolk Black
Narragansett	Slate
	Nebraskan Spotted
	Lavender

Eggs: Khaki Campbell, White Campbell, Abacot Ranger, Welsh Harlequin, Indian Runner, Magpie, Buff Orpington, Crested. Chinese geese. All turkeys.

Meat: Pekin, Rouen Clair, Saxony, Silver Appleyard, Muscovy, Cayuga, Magpie. Any geese. All turkeys.

Dual purpose: Blue Swedish, Silver Appleyard, Muscovy, Magpie. Pomeranian, Brecon Buff, Roman, Sebastopol geese.

Exhibition only: Aylesbury, Rouen, Bantam ducks. African, Toulouse, Steinbacher geese.

Weed control: All turkeys, most geese.

Slug control: Bantam ducks.

Insect control: All turkeys.

Appendix 2
EXPECTED EGG PRODUCTION
per year, mostly in spring/summer

Ducks

Abacot Ranger	250
Aylesbury	20
Bali	200
Black East Indian	15
Blue Swedish	150
Call	15
Campbell	300
Cayuga	40
Crested: large	150
miniature	30
Indian Runner	275
Magpie	150
Muscovy	50
Orpington	150
Pekin	40
Rouen Clair	40
Rouen	30
Saxony	150
Silver Appleyard: large	150
miniature	40
Silver bantam	40
Welsh Harlequin	250

Geese

African	15
American Buff	15
Brecon Buff	20
Buff Back	15
Chinese	40
Embden	15
Pilgrim	20
Pomeranian	20
Roman	30
Sebastopol	30
Steinbacher	10
Toulouse	10

Eggs: geese eggs are large and mostly white, duck eggs much smaller and either white or blue/green and turkey eggs are speckled and have a pointed end.

TURKEYS

Bourbon Red	50	Lavender	50
British White	60	Narragansett	50
Bronze	70	Nebraskan Spotted	50
Buff	60	Norfolk Black	70
Cröllwitzer (Pied)	80	Slate	50

Appendix 3
SHOW PREPARATION

This does not only mean having clean birds. Show Preparation starts months before a show because fitness (correct feeding for good bone and muscle) is the framework upon which all the superficial items such as feathers are built. Ducks, geese and turkeys are usually hatched in the spring when they naturally come into lay. It is possible to hatch some of them earlier if extra lighting is given to get them to lay earlier, especially if a particular show is chosen, but most of the major shows are in the winter by which time the young stock will have grown sufficiently and the old stock will have moulted out. The ducks with mallard type colouring can be a problem as they go into eclipse during the summer months and do not regain their breeding plumage until early October. Some heavy breeds do not mature until they are at least two years old, so will gain in breadth of body if the frame is there as youngsters. Even dark coloured birds need washing for a show. Either washing up liquid or baby shampoo is normally used. The birds are dunked in warm water, lathered, rinsed and dried either in front of a fire or with a hair drier or by putting them in a stable with clean shavings on the floor if the outside temperature is not too low. It is best to wash birds at least a week before a show to allow the natural body oils to return to the feathers. Put the birds in a clean show pen for a few days in an area with lots of human activity to get them used to the bustle of a show. If the birds are tame as well, then so much the better. Don't forget the legs, which may need scrubbing gently and be careful not to scrub the bill too hard as the top cuticle containing some colour may be removed. Birds with those feather colours that are liable to fade or change in strong sunshine tend to be kept in covered outdoor runs, which means they are still fit and still the correct colour. If you must wash a bird the day before a show, make sure it is dry before you box it as otherwise the feathers will stick out at all angles (like going to bed with your hair wet). Always try and use boxes that are too big so that the birds have enough room both to keep cool and to turn around which protects the tail feathers. Use a proprietary flea powder to make sure that none of these unwelcome parasites accompany your birds to the show.

All shows have an entry date which varies between several weeks before the show to one week before the show. Make sure you enter before this date as late entries are not accepted and check that your entries are correct for the various classes. Show Secretaries will give entry information if asked. Their addresses are in the *Poultry Club Yearbook* under Affiliated Societies, and lists of shows are usually published in the various poultry magazines. If you have shown the previous year, you will normally be sent a schedule. Make sure that your birds are penned in time for judging, and a little oil or vaseline rubbed on the bill or beak, wattles and legs will spruce them up. A silk handkerchief is said to be good for imparting a shine to the feathers, but the shine due to good feeding and management in previous months is more enduring.

Birds are not normally fed or watered in show pens before judging as this can change the correct outline or create dirt and droppings, but take food in the form of grain (firmer droppings) to a show plus water in a container suitable to pour through the bars of a showpen, as not all shows are of sufficient duration to afford stewards time to feed and water birds. Water containers are usually provided, but if in doubt, take either a two hook cup drinker or a small plastic container which can be wired, pegged or fixed to the pen so that it does not tip over. Bear in mind when returning from a show that dusting with flea powder is a sensible precaution, and ideally, all show birds should be kept separate from your other stock for a few days just to make sure that they have not brought something contagious home from the show, or that the stress of showing has not depressed their immune systems, allowing the entry of disease. A bit of cossetting after a show may well mean that a particular bird can be shown again soon, or return to the breeding pen in a fit condition.

Appendix 4
HOUSING AND MANAGEMENT

Housing is used by poultry for roosting, laying and shelter. The welfare of the birds is entirely in your hands and certain principles should therefore be observed.

Space and Water

Housing is needed for waterfowl and turkeys at night for safety from predators. Floor area should be a minimum of 2 square feet per bird for light ducks upwards, 3 square feet for geese and turkeys. Ideally, they will all be in a foxproof enclosure so will not need secure housing, especially as waterfowl see well in the dark and really do not like going into huts, except to lay. Make sure the huts have fairly high interiors so the birds feel less claustrophobic if they have to be shut in at night. A hut with a large entrance door, one that perhaps drops down, will encourage the birds to go in. Turkeys will use almost any type of hut suitable for chickens, as long as the perch is strong and not too far off the ground and the pophole is large enough for the stags.

Bantam ducks are going to need half the space of larger ones and do well in small enclosures with a pond or water container which is easy to clean and either on grass or gravel. If the area is foxproof, then a very simple shelter for laying in is all that is needed. Water for larger ducks can either be provided in movable ponds, thus avoiding the muddy patches which always accrue due to their habit of dabbling, or in a pond which is capable of being emptied from time to time for cleanliness. If a natural or dug out pond is very large, put small mesh netting around all the banks to prevent the waterfowl from digging them out as this is one of their favourite activities. Do not think for one minute that plants will survive in a pond with ducks. Unless it is a large pond and you have one pair of bantam ducks. Pea gravel around a pond will help to keep the area cleaner and this can be hosed down. No matter how disciplined you think you are, waterfowl acquisition is addictive, so allow for serious expansion when planning your enclosures.

Turkeys need a water fountain set off the ground to keep it cleaner.

Feeding

Use commercial feed for the correct species and age of bird and put this in vermin-proof hoppers. Hanging ones with a coiled spring at the base work well with ducks and wheat can be put in shallow troughs which are then filled with water so that crows and rooks do not eat the feed. Turkeys can either be fed from a hopper in their hut, or food scattered on the ground where they will enjoy searching for it, keeping them occupied.

Ventilation

It is vital to provide good ventilation as the thick feathering of waterfowl is all they need for protection from cold. It is to provide protection from predators that housing is used, not so much weather protection. Wire mesh windows or doors are best to allow good air circulation.

Nestboxes

Nesting areas for waterfowl are simple and consist of some wheat straw on the ground. Turkey hens will squeeze into impossibly small areas to lay and then have a habit of breaking the eggs, so make sure that a three sided nestbox is at least 18"x18" (45cmx45cm) with straw or shavings in it. A simple triangular hut with one side open is a good laying area for outside waterfowl as it affords some protection from aerial predators. Letting ducks out after 9am will ensure that 99% of the eggs are laid in the hut, as they lay at the same time every day. It is important to collect the eggs every day as the shells of waterfowl eggs are more porous than chickens' and thus bacteria can easily enter the egg. If wanted for incubation, the eggs should be washed in water warmer than themselves with a disinfectant such as Virkon in the water and then stored on damp sand at a temperature of 50°F (10°C) for not more than 7 days before being set. This increases the hatchability. If the eggs are left longer than 7 days, turning end over end is necessary and the hatchability reduces dramatically day by day. If the eggs are wanted for eating, they should be washed if dirty as above and then stored in the fridge at a temperature of not more than 39°F (4°C).

Perches

Waterfowl sleep on the ground and do not want a perch, except for Muscovies which do like to perch. Turkeys always need a perch, even from very young, but make sure it is broad enough not to dent the young and pliable breastbone – at least 2" (5cm) wide – and not too high off the ground (about 24" (60cm) is ideal) so that the heavy stags do not injure themselves when jumping down.

Litter

Wheat straw or woodshavings both on the floor and for nestboxes are the best materials. Do not use hay due to the mould organisms in it.

Floor

A floor of solid wood can be used, or preferably 1" (2.5cm) mesh as this helps with air circulation, and straw can be laid on top for waterfowl. Turkeys prefer a solid floor as this reduces draughts. Move all housing on a regular basis to help with hygiene.

Wing Clipping

The fully grown primary feathers are cut with scissors at the level of the small coverts on a young or adult bird. These grow back to full length the following year after the moult, usually late summer. Bantam ducks either need wing clipping, which has to be remembered to be done every year, or keeping in an aviary as they fly well. Birds are not usually exhibited with a clipped wing. Ducks larger than bantam ducks may occasionally need wing clipping if they persistently get over fences into other breeding pens. This is usually drakes of the Light breeds, see Appendix 1, Classification of Breeds, page 110.

Pinioning

At dayold, the final joint of the wing is removed with sharp scissors. There is little blood and the birds seem not to notice. This prevents flight for the rest of the bird's life. Bantam ducks are often pinioned as they are not only unable to fly, they can be exhibited in this state without penalty. Non-indigenous ornamental waterfowl must be pinioned as it is illegal to release them into the wild: in practice, all ornamental waterfowl are pinioned in order to prevent them flying away.

Sexing

Ducks and geese can easily be sexed by looking into the vent – males have a penis. The easiest times are up to 4 weeks old and after 6 months old. 'Adolescents' are difficult to sex by this method as it all looks the same. Ducks quack at 6 weeks old, drakes rasp. Turkeys need to be at least 14 weeks old to be visually sexed by size in the stags and markings in the hens. Vent sexing in turkeys is not an option for the hobbyist.

Appendix 5
COMMON DISEASES

Waterfowl and turkeys are relatively easy to keep healthy if a few basic principles are adopted.

Waterfowl

Intestinal parasites are the most common problem with waterfowl. Use Flubenvet either already in commercial pellets, or mixed in yourself, twice a year outside the breeding season for adult stock and from two weeks for young stock on grass, repeated every 4 weeks until they are 6 months old. If a duck or goose goes lame, worm it first before doing any other treatment, unless it is obvious that a bone is broken.

Lice can be a problem, but a good quality louse powder based on pyrethrum will remove these. If Northern Fowl mite get a hold, usually on the head of waterfowl, then Noromectin (Ivermectin) Cattle Pour-on (not licensed for poultry), 5 drops per bird, will remove these. These mites are tiny and dark red and spend their lifecycle usually on chickens.

Aspergillosis seems to affect waterfowl more than chickens. It is a fungus, so do not let litter go mouldy or leave rotting wood in waterfowl pens.

Mycoplasma can infect ducks as well as chickens, mainly the smaller breeds, possibly because their faces are foreshortened. The sinus needs flushing with Baytril plus an injection of Tylan 200 (not licensed for poultry) to control the organism in the rest of the body.

Coccidiosis can be a problem in young geese and ducks, but chick crumbs with a coccidiostat in should take care of this until the birds become resistant.

Angel wing occurs when too much protein is fed to young waterfowl. The weight of the growing wing feathers is too much for the immature wing joint, made weaker by an excess of protein, and the wing drops and then twists outwards. If seen in the early stages, binding up in a natural position with tape for 4-5 days will often work, plus reducing the protein. It usually occurs in large geese fed on chick crumbs for too long.

Corns can occur if insufficient water or too hard ground is in the pen.

Turkeys

Blackhead is a killer parasite disease which attacks the liver of turkeys. It is carried in an intestinal worm which inhabits chickens, so if the two species are kept together, regular worming of the turkeys will keep blackhead at bay. The affected turkey looks as though it has a hangover the first day. If treated with Emtryl in the water at this stage, the prognosis is good. Then the droppings turn sulphur-yellow the next day. It is less easy to cure once this happens, but if not spotted for 2 or 3 days, the turkey dies. Flubenvet is the wormer to use.

Lice are a common problem, treated with louse powder based on pyrethrum, but turkeys seem less inclined to be infected with mites than chickens.

Bumble foot can occur if perches are too high. This begins as a bruise to the sole of the foot and then becomes infected and swells into a hard abscess. Very difficult to cure if not caught early on and treated with antibiotics.

Mycoplasma infection causes foamy eyes and swollen sinuses. This is treated with an injection of Tylan 200 (not licensed for poultry) in the breast muscle. Again, if caught early on there is a greater chance of control. As turkey sinuses are much larger than chickens', sometimes an accumulation of hard pus can accrue. This may need removing if it impinges on the eye.

Wounds are always in evidence with any age of turkey as they are so keen on fighting. Dried blood looks black on the head (not the dreaded Blackhead) but will resolve after a few days.

Appendix 6
FURTHER READING

History and Management

Dr A. Anderson-Brown & G.E.S. Robbins, *The New Incubation Book* (1992, World
  Pheasant Association)
Chris Ashton, *Domestic Geese* (1999, Crowood)
Chris and Mike Ashton, *The Domestic Duck* (2001, Crowood)
British Waterfowl Association, *Waterfowl Standards* (1999, BWA)
Edward Brown, *Poultry Breeding and Production* (1929, Caxton) (3 vols)
Dr Clive Carefoot, *Creative Poultry Breeding* (1988, author)
Feathered World Yearbooks,1912-1938
Marsden and Martin, *Turkey Management* (1949, Interstate USA)
Victoria Roberts, *Diseases of Free Range Poultry* (2000, Whittet Books)
Victoria Roberts (Ed.), *British Poultry Standards* (1997, Blackwells)
W. Powell-Owen, *The Complete Poultry Book* (1953, Cassell)
Rev. T.W. Sturges, *The Poultry Manual* (1921, London)
W. B. Tegetmeier, *The Poultry Book* (1873, London)
Katie Thear, *Free Range Poultry*, 2nd ed. (1997, Farming Press)
Harrison Weir, *Our Poultry* (1902, Hutchinson) (2 vols)
Wingfield & Johnson, *The Poultry Book* (1853, London)
Lewis Wright, *Wright's Book of Poultry* (1919, Waverley)

Magazines (monthly)

Fancy Fowl, TP Publications, Barn Acre House, Saxtead Green, Suffolk IP13 9QT
Smallholder, Subscriptions Unit, Newsquest, 3 Falmouth Business Park, Bickland
Water Road, Falmouth, Cornwall TR11 4SZ
Country Smallholding, Fair Oak Close, Exeter Airport Business Park, Clyst Honiton,
Exeter, Devon EX5 2UL

Useful Addresses

The Poultry Club, Sec. Mr Mike Clark, 30 Grosvenor Road, Frampton, Boston,
  Lincs. PE20 1DB. (Hens, domestic waterfowl, turkeys)
The British Waterfowl Association, Sec. Mrs Rachel Boer, Oaklands, Blind Lane,
  Tanworth in Arden, Solihull B94 5HS. (Domestic waterfowl and wild waterfowl)
The Domestic Waterfowl Club, Sec. Mr & Mrs M. Hatcher, 2 Lime Tree Cottages,
  Brightwalton, Newbury, Berks. RG16 0BZ

GLOSSARY

Abdomen underpart of body from **keel** (breastbone) to **vent**

AOC Any Other Colour

AOV Any Other Variety

Autosexing breeds breeds developed where the males and females are sexed by colour patterns at day old or older

Back top of body from base of neck to beginning of tail

Balanced diet commercial ration necessary for correct growth and bone formation

Banding a line of a different colour to the feather going across it at the end of it

Bantam miniature fowl, one quarter the size of the large version

Barring two different colours going across a feather, each colour equal in width to the other

Beak the two horny mandibles projecting from the front of the face

Bean the tip of the **bill**, sometimes a different colour from the rest

Bill the beak of waterfowl

Breast front of a fowl's body from the point of the keel bone to base of the neck

Breastbone bone to which the major flight muscles are attached

Breed a group of birds answering truly to the **type**, **carriage** and characteristics distinctive of the breed name they take. Varieties within a breed are distinguished by differences of colour and markings

Breed Club an association of fanciers keeping a breed; most Clubs organise socials and send out Newsletters to their members who pay a small annual subscription

Broody the desire of a hen to hatch a clutch of eggs. She will fluff up her feathers and stay in the nestbox. She can be broken off by being secured in a small pen with food and water and out of the elements, with a wire floor for 14 days, or being allowed to sit for the usual 21 days to hatch fowl eggs in a quiet and dark place. If a duck or goose goes broody only let them sit for the usual 28 or 30 days as they lose condition fast. To break off waterfowl, move them to another pen.

Candling looking through the shell of an egg with a small but strong torch (in a darkened room) to establish fertility

Caruncles fleshy protruberances on head and wattles of turkeys and Muscovy ducks

Carriage the bearing, attitude or style of a bird, especially when walking

Chick a young turkey until it becomes a **poult**

Coccidiostat a drug put in the feed of young stock to inhibit the growth of the parasitic coccidia so that the birds have time to acquire immunity

Crest a topknot or tuft of feathers on the head in chickens and ducks. Compare with **tuft**

Defect either a deformity in any breed, or a deviation from the **Standard** for that breed

Dished bill bill with concave top line

Down initial hairy covering of baby chick, duckling or gosling

Drinker vessel to contain a reservoir of water, so designed that the minimum of muck or litter contaminates it

Dropped tongue in some strains of the larger breeds of geese, Toulouse especially, the tongue and/or food gets stuck in the skin of the lower mandible. It can be surgically corrected.

Dual lobe symmetrical pendulous area between the legs of geese

Duck footed fowls having the rear toe lying close to the floor instead of spread out, thus resembling the foot of a duck

Ears the ear canal hidden behind small feathers on the side of the head

Eclipse camouflage plumage acquired by the drake in the summer so that when moulting his flight feathers he is less conspicuous

Exhibition a type of poultry used for showing in competition, some of them having little laying capacity and therefore more often in their 'Sunday best' plumage than **utility**

Feeder container for feed which avoids contamination by muck or litter and may or may not be used for *ad lib* feeding

Flank the side of the bird, the thigh area

Flights see **Primaries**

Free range term to describe poultry allowed to wander at will

Frizzled curled: each feather turning backwards on itself so that it points towards the head of the bird

Graining the overlay of small (grains) amounts of a darker colour in plumage

Ground colour main colour of body plumage on which marking are applied

Growers term used for poultry from 10 weeks until they lay or are mature

Gullet the loose part of the lower mandible, the throat, the dewlap of a goose

Handling method of determining the correct body condition of a bird

Hardy the ability of some breeds to be productive in adverse weather conditions

Head comprises skull, face, eyes and **bill**

Heavy breeds a classification of heavier breeds, see Appendix 1

Hen a female after the first adult moult

Hind toe the fourth or back toe

Hock joint of the thigh with the shank

Housing see Appendix 4

Imprinting an identity survival instinct by a newly hatched duck or goose so that it can follow its mother, usually the first moving thing seen. If waterfowl are imprinted on humans, mating activity may also be transferred when adult which is a nuisance. Keep youngsters with others so that taming can still take place but the bird knows it is a bird.

Judge a person who has taken examinations in some or all of the seven sections of poultry, only one exam allowed per year, administered by the **Poultry Club**. There are four Panels: A,B,C,D, A being the highest qualification

Keel pendulous area below the **sternum**

Keel bone breastbone or **sternum**

Knob fleshy protruberance on upper mandible of certain breeds of geese

Lacing a strip or edging all round a feather, differing in colour from that of the **ground colour**

Laying trials in 1930s, breeds in competition, numbers of eggs laid in a certain number of days, plus weight and size of eggs. Done under scientific conditions at various agricultural institutions. Helped with selection for greater egg production

Leg the shank or scaly part

Light breeds a classification of breeds generally lighter in weight than the Heavy breeds, see Appendix 1

Litter wood shavings or straw as a friable basis in poultry housing and **nestboxes**

Lobe area between the legs of geese, see **dual lobe** and **single lobe**

Lustre see **Sheen**

Markings the barring, lacing, pencilling, spangling etc. of the plumage

Mealy stippled with a lighter shade, as though dusted with flour

Mossy confused or indistinct marking, smudging or peppering. A defect in most breeds

Pair a male and a female

Paunch area between the legs of waterfowl, see also **lobes**

Pencilling small markings or stripes on a feather over one of a lighter shade

Pin feathers new feathers coming through

Pinioning the act of removing the final joint of one wing when waterfowl are dayold to prevent them flying off when adult

Pipping the action of breaking the shell in one place by the chick before turning round, breaking the top off the egg and hatching out

Poult a young turkey until the sex can be determined at about 16 weeks.

Poultry Club an umbrella organisation for all keepers of poultry, whether **utility** or **exhibition**, guardian of the **Standards**. The members get four Newsletters per year, a Yearbook and the opportunity to partake in the annual National Championship Show (6,000 entries plus) in December

Primaries flight feathers of the wing, tucked out of sight when the bird is at rest. Ten in number

Quill hollow stem of feathers attaching them to the body

Rare breeds any breed not having its own **Breed Club**

Roach back hump backed, a deformity

Rump area just above the tail

Scapulars large feathers covering the shoulder area

Secondaries the quill feathers of the wings which are visible when the wings are closed

Self colour a uniform colour of plumage, unmixed with any other

Serrations sawtooth sections on the side of a bill

Sexing possible when waterfowl are up to 4 weeks old or after 6 months old by looking at the genitals in the vent. **Turkeys**: around 14 weeks the males have bare heads and thick legs

Shaft the stem or quill part of the feather

Shank see **Leg**

Sheen bright green surface gloss on black plumage. In other colours usually described as **Lustre**

Shoulder the upper part of the wing nearest the neck feather

Sinus the area between the eye and the nostrils. Can swell if infected

Single lobe area between the legs of geese with a central downward point

Snood the fleshy protruberance on the forehead of a male turkey which can be extended down in front of the face when displaying

Speculum a patch of iridescence on the **secondary** flight feathers

Splashed a contrasting colour irregularly splashed on a feather. In any blue breed when bred they produce blue, black and splashed progeny

Split crest divided crest that falls over on both sides

Sport an odd colour which may appear from a pure breeding pen

Spur a projection of horny substance on the shanks of males, small when young and getting progressively longer with age, and sometimes on females

Standard a precise description of all breeds, published in the *British Poultry Standards* (latest edition 1997and essential for exhibitors and judges. The **Poultry Club** is the guardian of the Standards

Stern area below the tail

Sternum see **breastbone**

Strain a family of birds from any breed or variety carefully bred over a number of years

Stub short, partly grown feather

Symmetry perfection of outline, proportion, harmony of all parts

Tail feathers straight and stiff feathers of the tail only

Tassel the very coarse hairs which protrude from the **stag's** breast. Sometimes seen on old female turkeys

Tertiaries the third rank of feathers in the wing

Thigh the leg above the **shank** and covered in feathers, see **flank**

Trio a male and two females

Tuft small feathers on the top of the head of a goose making a small bump. Compare with **crest**

Type mould or shape, see **Symmetry** and **Carriage**

Utility generally any breed of poultry which earns its keep by laying, producing meat or being broody. Not usually **exhibited** as they tend to be always in 'working clothes'

Variety a definite branch of a breed known by its distinctive colour or markings

Vent orifice from where either an **egg** is laid or faeces are produced, the two processes being entirely separate

Wattles the fleshy appendages at each side of the base of the beak, more strongly developed in male birds

Web a flat or thin structure as in web of feather or foot

Wing bar see **Speculum**

Wing clipping the cutting with scissors of the fully grown primary feathers of one wing to prevent flight

Wing coverts the feathers covering the roots of the **secondaries**

Wry tail a tail carried awry, to the right or the left side, a **defect**

INDEX

Page numbers in bold indicate illustrations.